how2become

How To Represent Yourself In Family Court

Michael Watson

Visit **www.how2become.com**
for more business titles and
career guides

Orders: Please contact How2become Ltd, Suite 2, 50 Churchill Square Business Centre, Kings Hill, Kent ME19 4YU.

You can also order via the e mail address info@how2become.co.uk.

First published 2013. ISBN: 9781909229525

Printed in Great Britain for How2become Ltd by:
CMP (uk) Limited, Poole, Dorset.

CONTENTS

CHAPTER ONE

INTRODUCTION

The representation of parents in the family court has long been the preserve of solicitors and barristers. If, as a parent, you were in conflict with the mother or father of your child and could not resolve the matter, you or your former spouse could take the matter to court and be represented by a solicitor via obtaining legal aid, which would pay for your solicitor's fees.

However, in recent years the accessibility to receive legal aid has become far more restrictive, which has led to many parents finding themselves 'between a rock and a hard place'. An increasing amount of parents are now in a position of either having to pay huge sums of money to their solicitor throughout the court case, or having to run the risk of attempting to go it alone and represent themselves in family court.

This is the predicament now facing the vast majority of parents who are in a dispute with the other parent, but are not wealthy or able to receive legal aid, and thus cannot afford to pay the level of legal costs incurred by the family court system. As a consequence, an increasing number of parents who feel they have no real choice are opting to go it alone with 'do-it-yourself representation'.

However, there are a host of factors that need to be considered and appreciated before deciding to take this route. For example, there are likely to be issues about your knowledge and understanding of the court process, your knowledge of the law, your skills and ability, your emotional state, and the support available to you.

Going to family court and representing yourself has got to be one of the most stressful, anxiety-provoking predicaments you could ever find yourself placed in. This is so for a variety of reasons:

To begin with, going to court is an alien experience for most parents. Second, the court is a very daunting place to be because you're under constant scrutiny. Third, the reasons for your attendance at court (i.e., your child) are extremely emotive. Fourth, you are unlikely to be in the best emotional state since most parents attend court shortly after a break-up with the other parent.

In addition to these factors, the vast majority of parents are simply not equipped with the knowledge and skills necessary to represent themselves competently at family court. Despite all these disadvantages, you are going to have to perform and present well, under what feels like intense scrutiny, in order to stand the best chance of achieving the outcome that you desire for your child or children.

Finally, what I would say is you have to appreciate that the court system is run on a very finite budget of resources. This means that the courts and Cafcass officers are under enormous pressures and, consequently, only allocate a short period of time to look at each case. Frequently, in practice, this translates to them of not having the time to look into your case with any degree of depth, and having decisions made that may not suit you or the other parent.

If I were to use the analogy that you are highly likely to experience the whole process (which can continue for many months, often as long as a year and sometimes much longer) as being on a ***knife edge***, I think that you will see my point (no pun intended).

Given this scenario, the odds then seem pretty heavily stacked against you as a parent being able to achieve the best results from the family court system. But, what if you were able to learn the required level of knowledge and gain the range of skills appropriate to give yourself the best chance of success without paying the small or large fortune that you'd be charged to be represented by a solicitor or barrister?

What if, also, having gained this knowledge and skills, you are in a real sense insured against ever needing a solicitor to represent you in the family court again? Having learnt what's necessary, in the event that you are ever taken back to court or conversely need to reapply to the family court, you are in a key position to take charge of your situation yourself, confident that you're now in a position to independently take care of your circumstances.

Well, that's exactly what **IS** possible. It is the subject matter of this book, and if you read on, you'll uncover a step-by-step guide, as well as practical support to give yourself the best chance of successfully representing yourself at court.

As an added bonus, in the process of acquiring the knowledge and skills mentioned above, you will also become a far better parent.

You are probably thinking that all sounds great, but I suspect you are also wondering just why you should be listening to me, and what makes me such an expert in this area of family court work, anyway?

WHY SHOULD YOU LISTEN TO ME?

This is always a sensible question to ask yourself when you are considering taking advice or guidance from someone. It invariably is prudent to find someone who has not only been through the experience or process you are about to face, but has done so several times, as well as coached or guided others successfully through the court process.

It just so happens that I have personally gone through the private law family court process and have experienced guiding someone very close to me through the process on numerous occasions, as well as having coached other people successfully throughout their court cases.

I should say from the outset that I am not a solicitor, legal representative, barrister, or anything like that. I am in fact trained in 'social work' and have over twenty-six years of experience in working with children, their parents, and families within the court setting. I have worked with large numbers of children and families within the public law court arena.

For those of you who do not know the difference between public law and private law, I discuss it briefly in the chapter titled 'Some Knowledge of the Legislation'. Very briefly, public

law involves a local authority taking a family or parent(s) to court due to concerns about the care of their child or children. Private law generally involves a dispute between estranged parents about aspects of how their child should be brought up.

So, how exactly does my experience and skills help you with your court case?

Well, quite apart from having over twenty-six years of working with children and families, I have been an expert in public family law proceedings for the past nineteen years.

What that means is that in public law when they want to assess whether a parent's care of their child is either 'harmful' or 'good enough', they would ask someone like me to assess a parent's capacity to care for his or her child.

Essentially then the courts would look to someone like me to make recommendations about where the child should live, who the child should have contact with and what frequency of contact a child should have with a parent, they would also ask me to assess what type of order would best secure the child's best interests. My assessment would cover areas such as (1) whether the parent(s) can meet the child's needs (2) what help the parents might require to meet the child's needs (3) what level of support or therapy the parents might need and (4) whether receiving this level of therapy and support they would be likely to improve the care of their child within the child's timescales.

To put it briefly, to be an expert in childcare and assessing parental capacity to care for children in the public law arena involves far more detail, complexity, and altogether more thorough work than the work of Family Court Advisers in private law cases.

Thus I am in a position to advise, guide, coach, inform, and support you to fully represent yourself, armed with the knowledge and skills you need to argue your case appropriately and cogently in court. With the information I can make available to you, the Family Court Adviser will find it hard not to be suitably impressed by your knowledge, skills, and care of your child or children.

In addition, as much of my work involves writing reports to the court and giving evidence at court, I am also able to support you with your statement and coach you to successfully negotiate giving evidence at court, as well as verbally representing yourself at court when not giving evidence.

I hope I have provided you with more than sufficient reason to listen to me and heed my advice. But if you still need further encouragement to do so, I can tell you that my years of work with the courts, solicitors, and barristers mean that I can also advise you on exactly how to conduct yourself at court, and how not to conduct yourself if you want to give yourself the optimum chance of achieving a successful outcome.

Finally, the skills you can learn will not only greatly prepare you for court, but also they will significantly improve your ability as a parent which will undoubtedly be priceless to you in the years to come.

Having a good relationship with your children is really of vital importance. One of the biggest regrets that many parents have, especially when advancing in years, is that they didn't take the time to invest in developing better relationships with their children.

I know! I know! I can almost hear you saying this is why you're having to go to court in the first place, to have a chance of seeing or spending any time with your child, but do not

underestimate the importance of learning the skills needed to be a better parent, as well as a better partner to the other parent.

Many people could have avoided going through the family courts if they had taken the time to learn how to be a better partner to your wife, husband, girlfriend, or boyfriend. I should also advise you that if there's any possibility you can save your relationship and avoid going to court, that you should most definitely try to do so. In the interests of clarity, my message to you is avoid court if at all possible.

CHAPTER TWO

ARE YOU CERTAIN YOUR RELATIONSHIP HAS IRRETRIEVABLY BROKEN DOWN?

Whilst this may sound like a really stupid question, it is necessarily one of the questions I am going to urge you to strongly consider.

I am going to encourage you to think seriously about your relationship with the other parent, because if there is any chance that you can repair or patch up your relationship, then I would advise you to do so.

Many relationships where reconciliation is a possibility break down because one or both parents choose to be inflexible or argumentative when cooperation and conciliation is what's required. If they continue on this path for too long, polarisation occurs and the opportunity for reconciliation is dashed.

Yet, it is not uncommon for ex-partners some time down the road to announce quietly, with remorse, that they made a mistake that they wish they could've rectified by resolving their differences and thus saved their relationship. Even if there is no possibility whatsoever of you and the other parent ever getting back together, it is still worth doing your utmost not to antagonise each other.

Quite apart from the fact that it's not necessary and potentially harmful to your child or children, it is sensible and wise to try to remain on reasonable terms with the other parent or as reasonable as possible under the circumstances. What I am really advising you about is that if it's at all possible, you can work out your differences without the recourse of the court, then it will invariably be in your interests and your child's to do so.

Going to court should be seen as the least favoured course of action for anyone who values a stress free, anodyne existence. In the event that the family court is the only option available to you, you are likely to need to negotiate a steep learning curve.

You are going to have to pick up a range of knowledge and skills swiftly. The first thing you will need is an understanding of what many parents, I believe, already think they have a very clear grasp of—that is, you are going to need to gain a clear sense of what constitutes good parenting.

CHAPTER THREE
GOOD PARENTING

Attempting to represent yourself in family court without a good understanding of what 'good parenting' is, and what it is not, is akin to trying to negotiate a very complex, long journey without a map or any other kind of navigation system.

As mentioned, most people probably think they have a pretty good idea what good parenting is and what it is not. But having worked with a great number of parents over twenty years, I have come to appreciate that your idea of good parenting is largely based around the parenting you have received yourself.

The spectrum of parenting styles is, in fact, extremely broad and your sense of what constitutes good or bad parenting is largely coloured by your own parenting or points of reference. So, for instance, some parents who have had, by most

people's standards, quite appalling childhoods may consider that they have had a 'normal' childhood.

Although that might sound crazy to you, if you think about it, it makes perfect sense because, for that person, their childhood and experiences were 'normal' for them. Even if you realised growing up that what went on at your home was not good for you, until you have lived with other adults or are mature enough to evaluate the parenting that you received with the parenting that other people received, you are generally not in a position to judge what value to place on your upbringing.

If you grew up in between warring parents or in an environment where you were subjected to verbal, physical, sexual, and/ or emotional abuse from your earliest age, why would you necessarily see anything wrong with behaving in that way, and why might you want to offer your child a better life, when no one thought of doing the same for you?

Even if you are consciously attempting to improve the care that you are giving to your child, if you have been subjected to abuse for a significant portion of your childhood, it is highly probable that your abusive experiences have become programmed or a habit that you no longer are consciously aware of acting out, such that you can be abusive without even being conscious of being so.

People operate from and behave according to the experiences they received as children, so that their experiences have become so much a part of themselves that they do not even think about it. This is equally true for you even if you have had good parenting experiences whilst you were a child. But however good your experience of being parented was, it could always be improved, even if only marginally.

There is no such thing as perfect parenting because none of us are perfect; we all have strengths in some areas and flaws or weaknesses in others.

The phrase 'good enough parenting' was said to be first coined by Donald Winnicott, who was both a paediatrician and psychoanalyst. He introduced the notion of 'good enough parenting' because it was recognised as unrealistic to expect parents to demonstrate perfect parenting.

Expectations of parenting that were close to perfection were unhelpful because they undermined the sterling efforts of many parents, who were in the majority of instances providing 'good enough parenting' to their children and enabling them to develop appropriately towards independence.

The idea of 'good enough parenting', although much more practical than the notion of perfect parenting, is, nevertheless, not clearly or easily defined and is perhaps more helpful as a concept than a strict set of principles or guidelines. Ideas about what constitutes good parenting, no doubt, have changed with the times and are culture specific, which again adds to the difficulty in defining what 'good enough parenting' or 'good parenting' is.

For the purposes of this book and assisting you in gaining a reasonably precise notion of what good parenting or good enough parenting is in the U.K. at this time, I will attempt to gather together the threads of what it entails.

WHAT IS GOOD PARENTING?

The first thing to say is that it is about being **appropriately responsive to your child and his or her individual needs**. Your level of responsiveness and actions will likely change, depending on the age of your child and what his or her needs and circumstances are at any particular time.

When your child is a baby you will be aware that your baby needs a substantial or intensive amount of care. A baby will need a lot of attention, affection, stimulation, and appropriate routines, such as being fed, cleaned, having one's nappy changed, and being allowed to sleep at set times, consistent with the baby's physical needs.

At the same time as the infant's physical needs are being met, if it is to develop appropriately, the baby will need to bond or emotionally attach to a main parent or caregiver. This is crucial in terms of an infant achieving a healthy and emotional development.

As a parent, whilst your baby is at this stage, you will need to provide intensive care to meet its physical and emotional needs well. As the infant becomes older and is less dependent on you, you will not need to provide the same level of intensive care, but you will still need to provide the baby with healthy physical routines to ensure they are eating healthy food regularly, and to keep a certain standard of hygiene, sleep patterns, and routines.

In terms of their emotional needs, you will need to be responsive and well attuned to the baby's feelings, wishes, and needs. As children become older, if developing properly, they will want to be more independent. This is appropriate, but although you will no longer have to provide the intensive level of care you did when your child was a baby, now you

have to understand and empathise with his or her needs and feelings whilst at the same time weighing up and making decisions about what you consider is appropriate or safe for your child to do.

Effectively then, you are still needing to be responsive to your child's needs, however, as your child becomes older, your decisions tend to become more complex because parenting or caring now involves holding your child's wishes and feelings in mind, whilst simultaneously looking at what you think is best for them, and yet at the same time, knowing that your role also involves preparing them for greater independence.

Demonstrating appropriate responsiveness then becomes more complicated as your child matures and involves balancing competing wishes and priorities.

WHAT ELSE DOES GOOD PARENTING INVOLVE?

It involves **consistency**. As a good parent, you have to be consistent at being responsive to your child's needs and meeting those needs on a regular basis.

Children will have a variety of different needs. For ease and for the sake of simplicity, I have chosen to differentiate their needs into either physical or emotional ones, though children also have other requirements, involving social, developmental, and educational needs.

But the most significant ones are the needs related to their physical care or health, such as eating, feeding, sleeping, being provided with suitable clothing, and having a safe and secure home environment. The other requirements are emotional needs which are concerned with your self-esteem or how you feel about yourself, identity, or self-image.

Whether you are happy or sad or are offered sufficient love and attention, as opposed to being neglected or ignored, and/or whether you have been exposed to abusive or violent behaviour as opposed to having a safe, stable, and nurturing environment are all matters contributing and connected to your child's emotional health.

To a large extent, if children's physical and emotional needs are well met, they are able to meet their other needs. But the extent to which their physical and emotional needs are well met will depend on how consistent their parents are at meeting those needs.

For your child to grow towards healthy independence, he or she will need to have been offered a consistent level of good care. It is of little value to a child to be offered the care needed only once in a while, when, in actuality, he or she requires it on a frequent and consistent basis.

Children who are offered inconsistent care can be said to experience a level of neglect of their needs, and probably will grow up to be less secure, stable, consistent, and contented adults. Linked closely to the important principle of consistency in parenting is the vital role played by providing children with **suitable routines**.

As documented earlier at the beginning of this section, babies and children require the provision of routines to help them to meet their needs and develop towards their potential. Routines, such as feeding, sleeping, changing their nappies, play and stimulation, enable your child to gain a sense of security and stability. Then they become accustomed to the routines which provide them with a degree of certainty, a sense of order, and reassurance about will happen next. In this way, children are able to make sense of their environment and the world. Good routines enable children to learn and make steady progress in all areas of their lives.

As well as establishing suitable routines for children that meet their needs, good parenting is about establishing **appropriate boundaries** regarding children's behaviour and offering them structure around who they are and what they should and should not be doing. But providing children with appropriate boundaries goes beyond regulating their behaviour, it also entails regulating your own behaviour as a parent and/or the people you allow to come into contact with your child.

Parents have countless opportunities to exercise appropriate and inappropriate boundaries with their children. Examples of setting inappropriate boundaries include calling the other parent a derogatory name in the presence of your child, shouting or swearing at the other parent in your child's presence, or using your child as a weapon against the other parent and/or telling your child that they will have to sort out the disagreements between their parents.

It also includes using your child as the means of communication between you and the other parent.

SO WHY ARE THESE EXAMPLES OF INAPPROPRIATE PARENTING?

Let me try to explain it this way: Your child loves both you and the other parent, and the other parent, like you, will be a significant and important part in your child's life long after you have finished caring for him or her. If your child loves you, how are they likely to feel, when someone calls you an unpleasant name?

To put it another way: if you love your parents or even someone unrelated to you, how does it impact on you when you hear someone else saying nasty things about your loved

one. Remember also that at this stage you are an adult, but your child is not. He or she is far more vulnerable, and your words can be very harmful to them.

Swearing about or at the other parent has the same impact as saying derogatory things about the other parent, and, of course, using your child as a weapon or instrument to hurt the other parent is definitely very harmful to your child. I invite you to recognise that by thinking about and acting out hurting the other parent; you can't help but hurt your child somehow in the process. As human beings, we are all interlinked and our actions have repercussions and consequences. And this is especially true of what goes on within your family.

In connection with telling your child that he or she will have to sort out the problems between you and the other parent, what I would say is that you have to bear in mind that your child is a *child*. Also never drag your child into the middle of the conflict by asking him or her to pass messages to the other parent. This means that they should not be placed in a position where they are being asked to take on **adult responsibilities**.

If you have ever had the misfortune of being placed in the middle of two parents at war with each other, you will know what I am talking about. Children need to be allowed to be children. They should not have to accept adult responsibilities until they reach a time when it's appropriate for them to do so. Even passing on little bits of information from one parent to another will expose them to the emotions and feelings of both of their parents.

One example of setting appropriate boundaries includes not allowing your new partner to stay the night and come into contact with your child, as you realise he or she is not ready to cope with the new person in your life and has not yet even

dealt with the loss of the other parent. Other examples might include not telling your thirteen-year-old child any information about their mother or father's infidelity, or remaining calm and not retaliating verbally or physically to the other parent's provocation whilst being observed or overheard by your child.

If you keep in mind that your child is a **child**, why would you want to expose him to adult issues before he is ready to cope with them? Your child does not need to hear that the father or mother was unfaithful to you. This might make them feel sorry for you or have the effect of making your child take your side in any arguments between you and your former partner. But it will never be anything other than harmful to your child overall.

I should perhaps add that encouraging your child to take sides, harms his or her relationship with the other parent, which is harmful and often has the effect of making your child overly worried about **you**. Children who worry too much about their parents rarely grow up healthy and frequently exhibit a range of anxieties, phobias, depressions or mental health issues in later life.

Keeping calm and stoical in the face of abusive treatment from the other parent is difficult to do, but it provides your child with the best example of how to behave during provocation. Essentially, this approach does not leave your child even more distressed as would inevitably be the case if he or she were to observe you retaliate.

Other examples might include being careful not to discuss issues with another adult about what the other parent has done to you, whilst there is any possibility of your child overhearing the adult conversation.

Further examples might involve controlling your feelings and body language, so as not to allow your child to pick up on

your negative feelings towards the other parent. By choosing to allow your child to have unimpeded contact with his or her father will create a healthier emotional environment for your son or daughter. Regardless of whether or not the father has paid you maintenance or irrespective of whether you are on good terms with him, your child's contact with the other parent should be valued by you, because it is important to your child. The only time you should seek to limit or stop the contact is if you are certain based on information you have heard from your child, or seen personally, that your child is being harmed as a direct result of having contact with the other parent. And the other parent has not taken steps to improve the situation.

Some parents (most frequently mothers) choose to limit their child's contact with their father if the father has failed to provide their child with regular maintenance. It is patently very hard to cope financially with a child, when as a parent you are not receiving the financial support you need, but this is where the old saying is applicable—'two wrongs don't make a right'. If you recognise your child's need to have a relationship with the other parent, you will value that need and let your child spend quality time with the other parent.

Obviously, the other parent should be contributing or doing his best to contribute to your child's maintenance, but that is his responsibility. In this example, **your** responsibility is to recognise the importance of your child's contact with the other parent and not seek to disrupt it by using contact as a bargaining tool.

Parents who offer their children appropriate structure and boundaries tend to be those parents who were themselves offered that same type of parenting from their parents when they were children.

Your children will by and large learn from you a sense of what is appropriate and what is not, depending on the experiences you show them throughout their childhood. It is, of course, possible to work on yourself and over time, with effort, alter the type of boundaries you would set or establish for your children. But how many of you either realise the need to do so or take the time to do so given today's hectic lifestyles?

Some of the most harmed or damaged children have been parented by parents who have offered their children no sense of personal boundaries whatsoever, to the point that their child has no sense of self or identity. In the example I am referring to, the child's parent(s) were so intrusive, never offering their child a sense of personal boundaries, such that the child grew up without any.

This child who happened to be male grew up with no sense of whether he was happy or not. He literally had no sense of being important, or of having any sense of self-worth. He did not know whether he was happy or sad because he had never been provided with an appropriate sense of personal boundaries from which to value himself.

Good parenting then has much to do with offering your child appropriate boundaries. By establishing these boundaries, you are really teaching your children about values, which enable them to value themselves as well as others.

If good parenting has to do with providing your child with a sense of 'good values' for themselves and for others, it's incumbent on you as parents to lead the way, or set the example by demonstrating to your child how you value them.

One of the principles of good or 'good enough' parenting is **prioritising your child's needs above those of your own**, or, in other words, placing your child's needs before yours.

If you intend to give your child the best opportunities in life to be happy and successful now and later as an adult, you will invariably realise the need to make sacrifices and to consistently place your child's needs in front of those of your own.

The mother or father who gets up five or six times a night when their baby is crying for some reason, does not do so, because their chief concern is about looking after themselves first and foremost. On the contrary, they do it because they recognise their child's needs are important, more important than their need at the time to get a good night's sleep.

Parents, who are able to consistently prioritise their child's needs in front of their own, frequently have been fortunate enough to have been brought up with good parents, who have demonstrated this value to them time and time again. It is precisely because they have done so that their grandchildren and great- grandchildren may reap the rewards from good parenting in the future.

One of the key or master skills to being a good parent is your ability to **empathise** with your child's wishes, thoughts, and feelings, and consistently keep those thoughts and feelings in mind.

Your ability to consistently place your child's needs before those of your own may be undermined if you do not possess the ability to see things from your child's viewpoint and remain well attuned to their needs.

Without the ability to empathise or remain tuned in to your child's needs, the chances of your child developing a secure bond of attachment to you (which is crucial during their formative years in order to develop properly in later life) are greatly reduced.

In terms of your child's chances of developing towards healthy independence, his or her failure to attach properly to you or another parent or caregiver will very likely have disastrous consequences for the child's current and future well-being. It is vital to a child's sense of safety, security, well-being, and the way he or she views the world to have developed a close bond of attachment to a consistent parent or caregiver in life.

If children are denied this close level of attachment during their formative or early years, they are much more likely to grow up seeing the world as cold and uncaring. They are much less likely to be able to empathise or show warmth to others, or respond appropriately to others' needs, since none was shown to them in their own childhoods.

In truth, there are so many aspects to what good parenting entails that hundreds of books have been written about it. For the purpose of providing you with a sense of what good parenting is about: I will conclude by stating that good parenting is about providing guidance and encouragement by setting examples your children will follow.

It's essential that parents come to realise that although children do not always do what you tell them to do, they, nevertheless, invariably imitate the behaviours or examples you have set for them. Unfortunately, much of the behaviour they imitate is behaviour that you as a parent may be unconsciously showing them, precisely because it is behaviour you, yourself, learnt from your parents, which was passed on unconsciously by them.

There is I would suggest a real need for all of us as parents (even those of you providing, in general, very good parenting) to become aware of what we are really exposing our children to when we behave rashly with only the concern to meet our feelings and needs above all else.

Good parenting involves taking the time and being open enough to question yourself; it is not about passing blame on to others, but is much more concerned with learning, being humble, and taking responsibility for our own actions.

As noted above, this is not intended as an exhaustive list of what good parenting involves, but I hope it serves to provide a fairly clear sense of what it entails.

Demonstrating good parenting is then not just about what we do or don't do for our children, it's about setting good examples and also about the way we treat, live, and communicate with the other parent. Being a parent of your child does not give either the mother or the father the right to make decisions without consulting the other parent and really thinking about what's best overall for your child.

Being a good parent means being willing to make compromises about certain matters and finding ways in which you can reach agreements. Although not exactly what either of you may have wanted, it means that your child receives some of the benefits that you both thought were important for him or her, and most crucially that your child does not have to see, hear, feel or experience living in a war zone.

Much of the problems parents get into with each other could be alleviated if more emphasis was placed on developing skills such as cooperation, listening, sharing, flexibility, putting the child's needs first, and focussing on reaching areas of agreement. These are some of the issues that may be addressed in mediation.

CHAPTER FOUR

MEDIATION

Mediation is a means of resolving disputes between estranged parents without going to court. It is an avenue suggested to parents in the hope that the problems can be ironed out adequately, so as to avoid the damaging and costly expense of embarking on the family court route.

Prior to commencing proceedings, parents in conflict are urged to consider seeing a mediator. They are qualified mediators who do not take sides and are not connected with you or the other parent in any way.

Their role is to attempt to allow parents an opportunity to meet with an individual who is appropriately trained, to help you both identify the issues and make arrangements or effective plans to address matters relating to your children currently and for the future.

The 'Mediation Information and Assessment Meeting' with your mediator will offer you an assessment of the situation and advise you as to whether mediation could alleviate or sort out your problems. The meeting is not lengthy, and if successful, it could result in saving you a substantial sum of money in court costs in the long run.

The cost of mediation is contingent on your personal circumstances, and if you have a very low income, it may mean that you need not pay for the meeting. The assessment from your mediator plays no part in the actual court proceedings in the event that mediation is unsuccessful in resolving your dispute.

Just go online to www.direct.gov.uk to find out where your nearest family mediation service is located. If you search for the words 'family mediation', you will be directed to a list of accredited family mediation services.

At the initial court meeting following the applicant making an application to the court, you may be offered a list of approved mediators from which to select one from.

APPLICANT OR RESPONDENT

You are the applicant if you initiate the court proceedings by making an application to the court, and your ex-partner or other parent of your child will be the respondent.

In order to apply, you can normally make an application by visiting your nearest court that deals with family matters. You should pick up or request a **C100** form, which is an application under the 1989 Children Act for a residence, contact, prohibited steps, specific issue Section 8 order, or to vary or discharge a Section 8 order. Depending on what

you want to achieve, your application may need to be started in a particular type of court.

For example, if you are a father and are making an application to be granted parental responsibility for your child, then you must begin your application in a magistrates' court. If you are the applicant you are expected to fill out at least three copies of the **C100** form and send them to the court.

Whether you are an applicant or a respondent, you need to be aware that you will both be the subject of a considerable amount of scrutiny throughout your family court proceedings, and this is one of the many reasons why I believe, whoever you are, you are going to need a substantial amount of emotional support.

EMOTIONAL SUPPORT

You may very well be wondering why this chapter has been included as an essential component or prerequisite for anyone in the process of attending the family court.

Whilst it may at first sight appear far less necessary than other chapters, anyone who has been through the family court system will likely testify just how crucial it is to be offered emotional support throughout the entire proceedings.

I would suggest that you think of emotional support as the glue that can hold you together and provide you with a secure and stable base, whilst you are subjected to on-going court proceedings, which could very well result in you experiencing one of the most stressful and daunting experiences of your entire life.

What I think you need to begin to realise is that you or any parent going to court (even if you have some experience of

court proceedings) are about to enter an arena of which you have very little knowledge. In fact, it is an alien and hostile environment, in which you are subject to quite a considerable amount of scrutiny at a time when you are highly likely to be emotionally less balanced due to the break-up of your relationship. Added to the likelihood of your emotional fragility is the fact that your conflict with your ex-partner involves your children, and there are few situations more emotive than how parents feel about their children.

Essentially then, what I would like you to bear in mind is that parents become involved with the court process, by and large, at the worst possible time in terms of their emotional and psychological wellbeing. Since they are simply not well placed to think things out as clearly as they might under different circumstances, neither are they in the best position to argue their case well or present it in the most positive light.

Frequently, parents need to vent their feelings and frustrations for a substantial period of time before they are able to be worked with to accept the guidance and support of others who may be better placed to offer them advice.

Your anger, hurt, frustration, and sense of injustice are what stops you from being able to hear and take advantage of good advice and/or to represent yourself more effectively. It is these emotions which need to be worked through and dealt with appropriately before you can hope to give yourself the best chance of achieving the outcome you want at court.

It will benefit you greatly to ask yourself questions such as these: If I were having to listen to parents in dispute, what would I have to hear which would fill me with confidence about their abilities as a parent? Conversely, what would I have to hear which would fill me with trepidation or anxiety regarding their abilities as parents?

Answering questions such as the above, thoughtfully and honestly, will provide you with invaluable insight into what you need to do, and how you need to present yourself in order to stand the best chance of gaining the result you want at court.

> The vast majority of parents come to court very angry with the other parent about a range of matters that have taken place in their relationship, much of which may bear no or little relevance to their court application or reason for being at court.

It will no doubt be of huge importance to you that the mother of your child has allegedly been unfaithful to you, for example. But this in itself will not be particularly important to those making decisions about your child, i.e., the Cafcass officer and the judge. If, on the other hand, you have evidence or information which suggests the mother of your child acted somehow inappropriately, resulting in your child witnessing or overhearing her mother's sexual activity, then this is information which is far more relevant to the court.

So why is the latter piece of information significant?

Obviously because it relates to your child, but more important, it is because it suggests that your child is being harmed by seeing or hearing behaviour which is not suitable for children to be exposed to.

At all costs, I would urge you to move away from the idea that the court is going to right the wrongs or perceived grievances you feel with regard to the other parent. Since the reality is that the court is not interested in what's gone on between the pair of you except for how it impacts on your child and how

it may do so in the future.

All you effectively do when you attempt to portray your ex-partner in a negative light, without being clear about how their behaviour, action, or inaction has been harmful to your child, is provide the relevant people with concerns about your suitability to care adequately for your child.

This is so because I would suggest you need to be aware that your negative feelings in relation to the other parent will invariably surface when you are with your child, and no child needs to hear 'bad' or negative things being said about the other parent. And conversely, your child also doesn't need to hear negative things about you.

When making statements about the other parent, it is also wise to be honest and provide the whole picture rather than to be selective with the information you provide.

For this reason, you may need the assistance of others to help you see the entire picture as it relates to your child and the role each parent played in bringing about the current circumstances.

In my experience, many parents often fail to recognise the part they've played in the break-up of the relationship and the resulting stress to the child. It frequently feels easier for parents to blame the other parent rather than to seek to take any responsibility for matters that have gone wrong.

It is also easy for friends and people who mean well to take your side and go on to demonise the other parent. This, however, is not helpful to you overall, although you may view it that way.

The type of emotional and practical support I am referring to acknowledges that no one's perfect, and that you will have

made mistakes that you need to learn from just as the other parent will have to do also.

Perhaps, it is necessary for me to state that even if you didn't cheat on your partner, were not in any way abusive to them or your child, but your partner cheated on you and was abusive to you and/or your child, you still have to ask yourself why you allowed it or put up with it for the length of time you did. Whatever the situation was in the past, you have to learn to accept your responsibility in helping to bring about the circumstances that exist.

Accepting your responsibility instead of seeking to blame others is something many people have considerable difficulty doing. The consequence is that the problems in your life and, most important, your children's lives can't and won't be sorted out until you figure out and address the matters that you are directly responsible for.

If you don't learn to become in a sense more humble and be open to the areas or ways in which you need to improve as the person and parent that you are, then you may not present in court the way you need to be seen.

Do not get me wrong, I am not suggesting that the other parent does not need to be more receptive and learn to accept their responsibility also, but you should not be concerned with them in this regard. If you want to achieve the best result you can, you will need to focus on your ability to learn what you need to learn.

There is often a tendency to see the whole thing as a bit of a competition, but I would advise you to instead focus on yourself in this regard only and accept your responsibility, or at least partial responsibility, for the current state of affairs, which are resulting in court proceedings.

It is vitally important to your application how you come across, so that you can achieve your desired outcome. This will happen if you have taken the time preferably with someone who can offer you critical and impartial advice to clearly think through what you are trying to convey and how best to say it.

Where possible you should attempt to stick to the facts and refrain from 'muddying the waters' with information that is not relevant to the matter at hand. It will not benefit you in any way to present yourself in an angry or unreasonable manner. If, for example, you are proposing that your child should reside with you, or have frequent contact with you, your case will not be assisted by verbally attacking the other parent or presenting yourself in an angry manner.

Why would anyone in their right mind sanction your child to live with you, when your actions are such that they leave those making decisions about your child to be concerned about your ability to remain focussed on your child's wellbeing, because it's obvious you remain livid about the other parent.

What needs to be kept at the forefront of your mind is that your actions, as well as your ex-partner's, are under continual scrutiny and need to be consistently seen as in your child's best interests (this topic will be further discussed in the chapter on legislation).

In essence, every move you make will or has the potential of being viewed through the lens of whether your action was harmful or beneficial to your child.

It may be beginning to dawn on you that your character, behaviour, and parental decisions are being judged or evaluated in quite a public arena. Although the proceedings and the records are confidential, a number of people in the court, including solicitors, barristers, Cafcass officer(s), court

clerks, and the judge will see or hear about your actions.

This is another reason why receiving emotional support will be so vital to any parent whilst in the process of court proceedings, because it may feel as though everything you do is being criticised.

In a sense this is inevitable because your ex-partner will seek to present their case in a way which portrays you in a negative light and will give rise to a certain amount of 'dirty linen being washed in public'.

Of course, this is exposing and embarrassing, but this I hope only serves to help you realise why it's so vital that you receive emotional support during the court proceedings. It is really an inevitable part of the court process, but you can exercise your individual choice about what you expose to the court, and I would always advise you to be cautious or circumspect when doing so. You need to think through how any information you bring up will ultimately portray you to those assessing you.

Frequently parents are willing to bring up things or matters which they anticipate will make the other parent look bad, without realising what it may also reveal about them and their behaviour. It's imperative that you recognise the court process for what it is. It is by nature adversarial (to an extent, it's inquisitorial) and exposing.

CHAPTER FIVE

AN UNDERSTANDING
OF THE COURT PROCESS

You do need to be aware that, although the wheels of the court do turn, in practice they tend to do so slowly for parents, who are anxious and desperate to resolve problems regarding disputes regarding their children. It is not unusual for the case to take up to a year and sometimes considerably longer to be completed.

The court process begins with one parent submitting an application to court, and leads to a first or initial hearing. At this stage, efforts are made to see if an agreement can be reached to solve or settle the dispute and many cases end at this stage.

But if this does not occur, there will be a further stage(s), which will include the parents filing their statements and the Cafcass officer completing their report to make a recommendation to the court.

At this stage of the proceedings, the case normally concludes following the Cafcass report and its recommendation.

If by any chance the case does not conclude at this point, it moves on to a final hearing, at which point both parents may be called to provide evidence under oath to the court and be cross-examined (i.e., asked a number of questions whilst in the witness box at court) by the opposing solicitor or legal representative.

The Cafcass officer may be called by one or both of the parents to answer questions at court regarding the report he or she submitted.

Once all the evidence has been heard, the judge then considers it and makes a judgement, which may or may not involve the making of court orders.

SOME KNOWLEDGE OF THE LEGISLATION

The main law that applies to your private law family case is the 1989 Children Act.

Private law as distinguished from public law relates to a private family dispute between parents or among family members relating to the interests of their children. This is opposed to public law which involves the local authority, such as Westminster City Council or the London borough of Haringey, taking parents to court regarding the care of their children.

I do not intend to provide you with a detailed account of the information contained in the Children Act 1989. Firstly, it is because you do not need a detailed account, and second, if you want more information about it, you can gain this online or from any good bookshop. What you do require is a very

brief summary of the main thrust of the act and some of the relevant terms and orders relating to your proceedings (in other words, Section 8 orders which will be discussed later in this chapter).

What the Children Act basically states, and what you, of course, need to keep at the forefront of your thoughts, is that your child's welfare is of paramount importance to the court. In practice, this means that your child's wishes, thoughts, and feelings are considered to be significant, and much weight will be placed on what your child wants.

It is vital that you understand this and recognise the value attributed to your child's wishes and feelings. The older in fact they are, the greater the weight or value will be placed on what they say they want and feel by the Cafcass officer and the court, up until the cut-off age of sixteen.

The whole thrust of the Children Act is to move away from seeing children as the possession of parents, and parents having rights in the absence of duties and responsibilities with regard to their children.

The Children Act introduces the notion of parental responsibility. In other words, that parents have rights as well as duties and responsibilities in connection with their children. It is their responsibility to make sure that their child's various physical, emotional, developmental, social, and educational needs are met until they reach an age when they are considered mature enough to manage their own affairs.

It is, of course, appropriate to talk with and consult your child's thoughts and feelings concerning decisions which affect them, and 'good parenting' would involve nurturing and guiding your child as they become older to take a greater responsibility regarding the decisions they face.

So, how do you find out whether you have parental responsibility for your child?

All mothers have parental responsibility for their children. The situation with fathers is quite different to that of mothers. Prior to December 1, 2003, in England and Wales, the father would only acquire parental responsibility automatically in the event that he was married to the mother. If he was not married to the mother, he could only acquire it via two methods: either by obtaining a parental responsibility agreement with the mother, or by being granted a parental responsibility order by the courts.

Married step-parents and civil partners may also acquire parental responsibility with regard to the child in the same ways. From December 2003 onwards, you will automatically obtain parental responsibility if not married to the mother, providing your name is on the birth certificate.

If your name is not on your child's birth certificate, you can still acquire parental responsibility through a parental responsibility agreement with the mother, or by being granted a parental responsibility order by the courts.

Parents with parental responsibility have the right to obtain information about their child's medical or health records and to give their consent or refuse to give their consent on behalf of their child regarding an operation or medical treatment.

A child's wishes and feelings are considered to be of significant importance to them, and thus are a reflection of their sense of wellbeing. It is for this reason that children's views and feelings are sought and whenever possible are adhered to, since it's believed that such action promotes their wellbeing and healthy development.

The Children Act also introduced the concept of harm when the various needs of children are being neglected or not met by their parents to the point that it can be said they are suffering harm. Harm can be defined as ill-treatment or the impairment of health and development, which includes for example impairment suffered by a child from seeing or hearing the ill-treatment of another.

Health refers to physical or mental health, which can also include emotional and/or psychological health. Emotional health involves having your emotional needs adequately met, so that you are able to feel good about yourself or your identity/self-image.

So, for example, a child who witnesses domestic violence or verbal or physical abuse from one parent to the other can be said to be suffering emotional harm. Because children suffer harm when they see or hear their parents being harmed, and this harm impacts negatively on their sense of emotional wellbeing.

This is because your child's wellbeing is (at least, when a child) inextricably linked to yours and the other parent's wellbeing, which is why when you harm the other parent or they harm you, the effect is to harm your child.

Children, like adults, have emotional needs, and you can talk about a child's emotional needs not being met when they have not been offered sufficient attention, love, and warmth from their parents. This includes when they have not been provided with the emotional security, stability, and consistency that they need, which would likely be the case if they have been subjected to observing or hearing their parents' domestic violence.

Impairment of a child's health and development refers to weakening, damaging, or injuring a child's health or

development. Development includes their physical, emotional, social, and educational development, and these different aspects of a child's development are generally interrelated.

People working with children often talk about a child's stage or stages of development. Generally children may begin crawling within six months and begin walking around twelve months. They begin babbling and talking at different stages or ages, and from these general stages professionals working with children gain a sense of whether a child is making 'normal' progress, is 'advanced', or is said to be 'behind' developmentally. Ill-treatment includes sexual abuse, physical, and emotional or psychological abuse.

Neglect refers to a form of harm which involves the persistent failure to meet a child's basic physical and emotional needs, which is likely to result in the serious impairment of their health and development.

The Children Act then seeks to promote children's welfare and wellbeing, and limit or reduce their chances of suffering harm.

As it is acknowledged that the vast majority of children are distressed by their parent's conflict (resulting in court proceedings), and that their attendance at court will give rise to further upset and trauma, children are rarely urged to attend court.

Even in those instances where children, who are normally teenagers, say they want to attend court, it is generally discouraged since the court recognises how daunting and distressing attending court can be for adults, let alone children.

No doubt it has begun to dawn on you that your children have a considerable amount of influence over the final outcome at court, especially if they are over the age of ten or

eleven. For this reason, there is a potential for some parents who have no scruples to attempt to manipulate, control, and unfairly influence their child's views such that they cooperate, comply, or align themselves with whatever the unscrupulous parent wants.

However, this is a very dangerous game to play for three main reasons:

1. This course of action can backfire, in that it may become obvious to the Cafcass reporter and the judge that you have abused your position. As a result, this makes it clear that you are not a parent who can be relied upon to be honest and act in accordance with your child's interests and wellbeing.

2. What I think is far more important is that if you have no qualms about behaving in this way, it is highly likely that you have done so before. Consequently, the cumulative impact over time of your care or parenting of your child will have a disastrous long-term effect on your child's development and wellbeing.

3. Your actions will not only damage your child's wellbeing as an adult, but it will also inevitably damage your relationship with them in later life.

Parenting is never a simple or easy matter, but all reasonable parents need to distinguish between what their child needs in terms of care, attention, and guidance, balanced against your child's need to be able to freely express their wishes and feelings. The older they become, the more important it is that they are encouraged to express their feelings and for their views and wishes to be valued and respected.

Essentially as a parent, you will have to choose whether your child's needs come first, or you put your needs in front of

theirs. Good parents place their child's needs before those of their own.

Along with the new principles and terms of the act, the Children Act refers to the ***Welfare Checklist***, which is essentially the criterion by which the court judges a child's welfare and best interests.

The Welfare Checklist is as follows:

- The wishes and feelings of the child in light of his age and understanding.

- The child's physical, emotional, and educational needs.

- The likely effect on the child of any change in their circumstances.

- The child's age, sex, background, and any characteristics the court considers relevant.

- Any harm the child has suffered or is at risk of suffering.

- How capable each of the child's parents (and any other relevant person in relation to whom the court considers the question to be relevant) is of meeting the child's needs.

- The range of powers available to the court.

In addition, there are court orders of which any parent who needs or wants to represent themselves in court will need a brief understanding. However, before turning to look at them, it's necessary for you to understand another principle of the Children Act.

The principle I am referring to is called 'The No Order Principle', in other words, the court has to weigh up and be sure that it only makes an order when to do so would be better for the child than making no order at all.

This is a guiding principle that the court should always consider when considering whether to make an order or not.

The Section 8 Orders of the Children Act relating to private law family cases are as follows:

- Residence Order
- Prohibited Steps Order
- Specific Issue Order
- Contact Order

A Residence Order determines who your child lives with and where they reside or live. If granted a residence order, you also receive parental responsibility if you did not have it previously. This will mean that you continue to have parental responsibility for your child or in respect of a child until the child reaches sixteen, when the order ceases to be in effect.

In exceptional cases, the court may decide that the order should continue until your child is eighteen.

The act of granting you a residence order does not mean that those who previously had parental responsibility have now lost it. They continue to hold parental responsibility, but their ability to exercise it is curtailed if the child no longer lives with them.

If the court grants you a residence order, it means that you will be allowed to take your child abroad for up to one month without seeking the permission of the court or others who have parental responsibility.

You will not be able to change your child's surname, nor should you be so minded to consent to your child's adoption, without the agreement of all those holding parental responsibility with regard to your child.

Residence Orders allow those who are not the legal parent of a child to gain parental responsibility in relation to them, such as an unmarried new partner of one of the child's parents or a previous partner of a parent with whom the child spends much time with, such as when there is a shared Residence Order.

Shared Residence Orders at one time were only granted when the parents were thought to be able to cooperate with one another. However, this has now changed, and the courts are now much more prepared to grant shared residence orders where they consider it appropriate.

It is perhaps important for me to state that courts are advised by Cafcass officers, and that what Cafcass officers may consider appropriate may appear highly inappropriate to both parents for whom cooperation has long and irretrievably, broken down.

Shared Residence Orders do not necessarily mean, as is often thought to be the case, that both parents are offered an equal amount of time with their child. In fact, any combination or ratio of times can be recommended and agreed by the court.

Matters such as the parents' work schedules, the distance between the parents' homes and the school your child attends, as well as their wishes and feelings, are all factors, which need to be taken into account.

How does the court decide where and with whom your child should live?

This decision is considered to be arrived at by the court taking your child's age, wishes, needs, and welfare into account.

A Prohibitive Steps Order is an order which prevents one parent from taking a specific action in relation to the other

parent's exercise of parental responsibility. So, for instance, one parent may apply to the court to grant a PS Order to prevent the other from taking their child abroad or coming into contact with the other parent's partner, who he or she considers poses a risk of harm to their child.

Anybody with parental responsibility, a Residence Order, a guardian or parent can apply for a Prohibited Steps Order. Other people can only apply following the court granting them permission to do so.

A parent or guardian applying for a PS Order will need to fill in a C100 form and write a Position Statement which will need to be presented to the court.

The Position Statement should be as clear and succinct as possible, outlining both the reasons for your application and why the making of the order would be in your child's best interests.

The consequences for breaching a PS Order could result in the parent concerned being prosecuted, and could even result in them receiving a custodial sentence.

In the event that a non-resident parent takes their child out of the country without the court's permission, there are actions which can be taken to recover the child, but this very much depends on which country the child has been taken to.

As I understand, as of 2012, there are forty-five countries that have entered into an agreement with the U.K. concerning the recovery of children removed by a non-resident parent from the court's jurisdiction without their consent.

In carrying out its duties the court will look at the relationship between the child and the applicant (i.e., the person applying for a PS Order) and make a decision regarding its appropriateness. The court will also ponder any risk of harm

that may accrue from the application impacting on a child's life in such a way as to cause him or her harm.

A Specific Issue Order can relate to any issue the court is asked to decide concerning a matter of parental responsibility. Frequently, these applications are made to the court to resolve issues such as a child's education, religion, receiving an operation, or deciding whether the child can go to live permanently in another country.

Any parent or guardian of the child or person with parental responsibility, including the child or his siblings, relatives, or even medical practitioners can apply for an SI Order. In fact, anyone who claims an interest in the child in question can seek an SI Order. The court, in carrying out its duties, will always be guided by the paramount consideration of whatever it considers to be in the best interests of the child.

Any applications for an SI Order will be heard before a Cafcass officer and at this meeting they will try to reach an agreement between the parents to resolve the issue.

If this cannot be achieved, the next step is normally for the parties (i.e., the parents, their solicitors, and the Cafcass officer) to arrange 'Directions' for a trial. Prior to the trial date, the parents will normally produce statements they intend to rely on, and the Cafcass officer after seeing the parents and the child, normally together, will have interviewed the parents to provide a report and recommendation to the court.

The judge invariably follows the recommendation of the Cafcass officer. On those rare occasions when judges depart from their recommendations, they explain and give reasons why they have done so.

In the majority of cases, the case does not progress beyond this point, but if it does, there will be a full hearing in which

both parents may be required to give evidence at court under oath and be cross-examined by solicitors or barristers from the opposing side.

A Contact Order is an order stipulating that the resident parent provides contact (which used to be known as access) to the non-resident parent at a frequency named by the court. If the resident parent is not allowing you to have contact with your child or is sabotaging or providing you with very inconsistent contact, and there is no way you can agree on a way forward, then you may have to go to court to apply for a Contact Order.

However, it should be noted that many parents (fathers, in particular) are granted contact orders, but may still fail to see their child regularly in the event that the resident parent, often the mother, fails to comply with the contact order.

In practice, it is very difficult for the court to resolve the issue of intransigent parents. The last thing that judges want to do is to give the resident parent a custodial sentence because of the harm and disruption it inevitably causes the child.

However, in exceptional cases where the resident parent is thought to have a personality disorder (narcissistic personality) or some form of mental illness, courts have been known to place the child with the non-resident parent.

Mostly, the situation is not resolved, and parents feel forced to take the matter back to court again and again. This, of course, is a highly distressing and unsatisfactory situation, but it is a situation that you as a parent need to be aware of because obtaining the order does not necessarily provide you or your child with any certainty that you will receive the contact you expect.

Often the court and the Cafcass officer hear two different

stories from the parents about what has happened, and they simply don't know who is telling the truth. This is why I would say that it is in your interest to present information at court (verbally) and in your statement as factually as possible.

FACTS AND OPINIONS

It is very important when presenting information at court, either orally or in writing via your statement, to make your account as factual as possible and to avoid speculation. The court does not want to hear what you think happened or is happening; they want to know the facts.

Factual information is backed up and supported by evidence and is thus verifiable. Opinion, on the other hand, is simply what you think, what you suspect, or what someone has told you has happened. Opinions are really your beliefs; they are not necessarily correct and may not stand up when considered in the light of objective scrutiny.

It is advisable to keep your beliefs to yourself, unless you have fairly strong independent evidence which supports or corroborates your views. You have to try to remain aware that, like most of us in such predicaments, you are not your most rational and balanced self at this time of your life. After all, you have experienced a recent break-up and have become engaged in a dispute over your children at court.

Under such circumstances, it is very easy to jump to conclusions, which may have very little if any truth to them. Even when you are more emotionally balanced, and when you have or are presented with only a snippet of information, your mind is inclined to want to fill in the missing pieces in the absence of facts.

For this reason, it is really important for your sake in terms of how you are viewed at court that you take the time to develop an enquiring mind, not just about what others tell you, but also in relation to your own thoughts and beliefs.

Keeping an open mind about things is not always easy, but unless you try to do so, you can easily come across as being judgemental, bitter, or just unbalanced. None of which sends out the type of message you wish to give to the Cafcass officer or the court.

Just try to bear in mind that there may be a whole range of reasons why certain things are done, or your children, for example, behave in a certain way. Jumping to conclusions on the basis of limited information is unlikely to prove to be helpful.

Gossip, rumours, and innuendo are examples of hearsay information and are not valuable or reliable as evidence; they do not become elevated to that of reliable factual information until or unless they can be adequately verified. A fact is not open to interpretation or debate in the way opinions are. A fact is neither ambiguous nor unclear; it is certain and definite.

In private law family proceedings, one parent will often provide one version or account of events, whilst the other will state that it happened in a totally different way. Whilst the court will not take the time to investigate fully what the truth of the matter is, the closer your account can be seen or recognised as being factual, the more trustworthy you will appear.

You do need to be aware when submitting information to the court, either verbally or in writing, that you are mindful of ensuring that you, yourself, have not jumped to conclusions

or made assumptions and interpretations which undermine your credibility and judgement.

WHAT ARE STATEMENTS FOR AND WHAT SHOULD GO IN THEM?

When it comes to writing your statement, this is one of the areas in which some parents can feel out of their depth. It depends to a large extent how comfortable and confident you are about writing and arguing your point in the form of a statement.

If you are one of those people who didn't do well in English at school, who never felt they were any good at it, or for whom English is not your first language, it is totally understandable that for you writing a statement seems a huge obstacle you can't get over or around.

Even people who were very good at expressing themselves via writing can see this as a very big challenge.

But trust me when I say to you, this does not mean that you will not be able to write a statement for your family court case!

From this point onwards, the word 'can't' no longer exists!

You can do whatever you put or turn your mind to.

Will it take time to be done adequately?

Will it require a lot of your effort and determination?

Might it require the help from other people?

Might you have to practice doing it over and over before it reads well?

Could you be shocked in the end by how well you have overcome that massive obstacle?

The answer to all of those questions is YES.

It will take your time, determination, effort, help from others, constant practice—and yes—you are probably going to have to sacrifice watching your favourite programme or doing something else you like.

You won't achieve your desired result by giving nothing in return.

But let me ask you a question: Isn't your child worthy and deserving of all of your strenuous efforts?

If the answer to that question for you is 'no', then my question to you is, what are you doing reading this book?

The only real reason you are reading this book is because your child means everything to you, and you want the opportunity of playing a useful and important part in their life and in maintaining and developing a fruitful and positive relationship with them throughout their life.

If you are reading this book for any other reason, you will be doing a major injustice to your child; you are very likely to harm them; you run the risk of jeopardising your court case, and, in the long run, your actions will harm you.

I CANNOT EMPHASISE THIS POINT STRONGLY ENOUGH

If you are going to the family court to victimise, abuse, punish, or hurt the other parent, or your actions and intentions regarding your child are fuelled by rage and hate, there is no good outcome that can stem from this. And you would be better off spending your time with a counsellor, therapist,

and/or receiving all the emotional support you can, to rid yourself of your toxic thoughts and feelings.

I urge you to examine your feelings and motivations. Wherever your intentions are not solely centred on what's in the best interests of your child, I encourage you to take your full responsibility for altering the circumstances and improving the situation for your child's benefit and ultimately your own.

The old saying is true 'You reap what you sow'.

Now let's turn to look at what your statement should be about.

Your statement is your opportunity to tell the court in a documented form your view of the background or history of the case.

It may be that your ex-partner has painted a picture of you as historically behaving in an abusive, threatening, and unreasonable manner to them and your child.

Then this is your chance to set the record straight or explain your account of what has taken place between both of you and with your child.

It is important to remember that you need to place your child's feelings and wellbeing at the centre or focal point of your arguments. If you have been accused of behaving badly or without regard to your child's feelings, it is essential that you address the points and show why this was not the case.

If the events described by the other parent were for the most part true, then acknowledge it. It is far better that you acknowledge it and make it known, and that you have taken steps to learn or address any shortcomings, than try to deny it.

One of the worst things you can do is consistently fail to accept when you have behaved without consideration for

your child's feelings, especially when it is obvious to those observing you.

If you can't accept where you may have gone wrong, you will not take your responsibility for your failings and are likely to continue to behave as before.

If you are able to accept where you have gone wrong, it provides a far better impression and likely impetus or motivation to do better in the future.

Your statement should also provide the court with your view of what is best for your child, and how you propose matters should move forward.

When making your proposals about what is best for your child in terms of, for example, where and with whom they should live, who they should have face-to-face and phone contact with as well as the frequency of such contacts, which school they should attend, or whether they should be brought up in a particular faith, your arguments should take into account a range of issues.

These issues can include a broad spectrum of questions: Who is your child emotionally attached to? How often are they used to seeing the non-resident parent? How upset are they likely to become if this is altered in any way? What are your child's routines and homework schedule? What clubs or other activities is your child regularly engaged in? What particular characteristics or special needs does he or she have? Does their personality or level of intelligence indicate that they would benefit from a particular type of school? How socially conscious and spiritually aware is your child?

It is your duty to take the time to think about exactly what your child's needs are. This is where you might realise the

benefit of developing your parenting skills as was discussed in the chapter on 'Good Parenting'.

Being able to empathise with your child's needs and feelings, and to prioritise their needs in front of your own is crucial.

You need to consider their emotional needs: Who are they closest to? How easily do they become distressed under certain circumstances? How resilient are they after being let down? Have they been starved of affection or attention? Do they have issues regarding their self-esteem?

Thinking about their physical needs is important: Are they healthy? Do they have any type of disability or require any particular type of care or medication? Are they susceptible to any kinds of illnesses, allergies, or conditions? Do they have problems with their sleep or appetite? Have their physical needs been neglected in the past such that they need consistent and better care in the future?

You'll need to reflect on their educational, social, behavioural, and developmental needs: Have they or are they being offered the opportunity, encouragement, and stimulation they need to progress? Are there concerns about how they relate, play, engage, take instruction, and cooperate with peers and people in authority? Are there concerns about either their ability to be managed in school or to have control of their anger.

If you think carefully about who your child is and what their various needs are, you should be able to produce a well-framed argument about what is best for your child. You need to remain focussed on their needs, not yours, and weigh up the competing or conflicting needs, giving priority to those needs that are most important in terms of their health and wellbeing.

In general, you should aim to make your statement as concise as possible, and seek to avoid displaying vituperative remarks about the other parent, irrespective of whether they are making unpleasant remarks about you.

If you train yourself to stop thinking about what you want or thinking about the other parent, and just keep maintaining your thoughts on your child's wants and needs, you will be less likely to say things that will jeopardise your chances of success and more likely to present yourself positively on paper.

If you read over and edit your statement properly, you will cut out things you perhaps don't need and make your statement clearer, more succinct, and easier to read.

Just imagine what it must be like having to read really lengthy accounts, which are full of vitriol and monotony.

Judges and Family Court Advisers are only human after all and can swiftly become jaded, and, consequently, less willing to see you or any worthwhile points you may make in a positive light.

So, by all means, explain the history, your child's needs and feelings, but keep it short and to the point. Try to make it no more than about five pages; if you can make it a lot less, do so provided that you cover the points you wish to.

Explain how long you and your ex-partner were together, why you broke up, particularly, if it relates to your child. Describe the circumstances of your relationship if relevant, who played the major part in caring for your child and the reasons why this was the case.

Mention any other significant issues about your child, particularly, if they have a bearing on the matters of contention

between you and the other parent. If your child clearly wants to see you or see a lot of you (in the event that you are not being allowed to see your child by the other parent), state this, and explain both why this is so, and, as clearly as you can, how distressing that is for your child.

If, on the other hand, your child is saying they do not want to see you, this could be for a range of reasons. Do not automatically jump to the conclusion that the other parent has turned them against you. Although this is possible, you probably played a part in this even if you are not conscious of the part you played.

It may be that your child, depending on who they are and their stage of development, sees you as betraying their trust and the other parent's trust in you. Perhaps, you had an affair, or presented the other person as a friend, and they later discovered them to be the person that you are or were having a relationship with.

Under those circumstances, it's easy and convenient to blame the other parent for allegedly turning your child against you. What, however, is harder to do and yet absolutely vital to your relationship with your child is to take responsibility for your actions and the part you played in the current situation.

If your child consistently says they do not want to see you, it's never wise to express the view that your child should be forced to see you. The Cafcass officer and the court are highly unlikely to sanction this in any case, mostly because it will feel abusive to your child and will very likely have a counterproductive impact, strengthening their resolve not to see you, currently, and in the future.

The most sensible thing you can do under these difficult circumstances is to really reflect and consider how this

situation has come about and the part you played in it. Address this issue, if you discover what they are upset about via letter, phone, or any other agreed or acceptable way of communicating with your child.

Do not be tempted to try to contact your child via secretive or underhanded methods, and make sure your behaviour can be seen as open and transparent.

When I suggest that you address this issue, which does not mean trying to sweep things under the carpet. If you can see that you are wrong, be adult enough to acknowledge it and take responsibility for putting things right.

Try to remember the family court is not about punishing you for your past indiscretions, no more than it is about praising you for your past or current good behaviour. It is simply a process, which has a system it uses to decide what should happen as regards to your child.

Being wrong in the past doesn't mean that you will not be viewed as having a valuable part to play in your child's life currently and in the future.

So, if you can demonstrate that you have accepted where you have made mistakes in the past and now intend to consistently put things right, it is to your advantage.

The sad reality for a lot of children is that their parents are unable to accept where they are wrong and are more interested in laying blame elsewhere than taking their responsibility for resolving situations properly.

Be open about what you may have done in the past and what you have learnt. Inform the court via your statement that you will continue to be consistent regarding requesting reasonable contact with your child. Be prepared to be very

flexible regarding contact, since what you want is your foot in the door 'so to speak'.

In the event that you are offered contact with your child, at all costs, ensure that you are on time and behave appropriately throughout. This means do not do anything which gives anyone the opportunity to claim that your contact should be stopped.

In your statement, if relevant, explain exactly who your child is: talk about the type of personality they have, and how the conflict is affecting them, and what you have attempted to do to reduce their stress and upset.

As already stated, you will achieve the best results by articulating your view(s) in accordance with what's consistent with your child's needs or overall best interests.

For instance, let's say you are the resident parent and the non-resident parent (father) is seeking overnight contact from Friday night to Sunday for two weekends of the month. But you know that your child, aged six, has never spent more than three or four hours in his father's care at one time, has certainly never stayed with him overnight, and is used to his routine at home.

Under such circumstances, you might want to explain what your child is used to, and what the affect on him would be from having his routine disrupted.

Presuming that you are not against your child having some contact with his father. If he is comfortable with his father for some three or four hours at a time, you may want to argue that you'd be happy with the father commencing contact for about a four-hour period in the day on Saturday or Sunday, but that you object to more than this until your child is ready for a longer period of contact.

It would be wise in my opinion to explain that your six-year-old son is still very attached to you (if that's the case), and how upset and distressed he becomes when separated from you for too long a period.

You might want to suggest that the father brings him home to you or that you rendezvous at a meeting point before it gets too late in the evening, so as to ensure that your child's evening routines are not disrupted. Then your child can have his meal, can wash up, and get to bed at his usual time.

If your child has a routine of getting in bed by 7:00 p.m. or 7:30 p.m., you might want to suggest that contact takes place between 12:00 p.m. and 5:00 p.m., so that your child is home in time to maintain routines he is accustomed to.

You would in a real sense be testing how your child copes with being away from you and being with his dad for a slightly longer period than usual, and you should be explicit in stating that if your child shows no adverse affects, then you will consider increasing the contact slowly. On the other hand, if he displays signs of distress or disturbance, you probably would rather keep it at that level or a lower level for the time being.

This demonstrates your flexibility, and that you are not just being obstructive concerning your child's contact with his father.

Thinking about your child's needs such as his routine and his attachment to you, and how upset he becomes when out of your company for many hours, shows that you are considering your child's feelings. But you also have to demonstrate that you are aware of and have thought about what your child says he wants, and you recognise the need for your child to have contact with his father.

Your argument will have to address whatever your child says he wants, even if what he says he wants conflicts with what you are sure is in his best interests.

For example, although your five-year-old daughter may not cope well with being away from you for more than three or four hours, she may still say that she wants to see her dad for the whole day.

Your job then will be to explain how distressed she is likely to be in practice if she is allowed to spend the whole day with her father at this stage. It would be wise to argue your case via using examples which show how she has behaved in other similar circumstances before, and if possible, cite or give the names of others who have witnessed your child's distress.

Your arguments will hold more weight if they can be backed up by others, especially people who are seen to be impartial. Such people could be school teachers, health visitors, nursery aides, nurses, etc.

In the event that you are not happy with the father having contact with your child, you need to be very clear why you oppose his contact.

The family courts generally work with the expectation of the presumption of contact with the non-resident parent, because it is believed that this is best for your child.

This means that if you are going to be successful at stopping the other parent from having any contact with your child, you must have really compelling reasons why he (though it could be the mother) should not have contact with your child.

I will say it loud and clear:

> **The only reason you should be attempting to stop the other parent from having contact with your child, who is both yours and the other parent's, is if they have in the past and/or are actively harming your child or you in some way.**

If the father is physically, emotionally, or sexually abusive to your child, or is abusive to you in any of the ways mentioned, including psychological abuse, controlling behaviours or constantly belittling and undermining you, these are the types of behaviours which justify you in trying to stop the other parent from having contact with your child.

If the father is doing any of the above to you, he is not just harming you, but also your child as your child will inevitably see, feel, and experience your upset, fear, or harm in some way.

However, you will have to prove or provide good evidence to demonstrate the harm he exposes your child to, which is frequently far from easy, given the court system which exists.

If, by any chance, you have corroborating evidence, for example, from your doctor, neighbours, or a neutral person, who has witnessed the other parent abusing you or your child and is prepared to provide corroborating evidence that you can attach or appendix to your statement, this would be very helpful to your case. Or, if you have proof in terms of photographs or documented contact with the police or authorities, this may be very useful.

But what if you are a non-resident father being prevented from having contact with your son or daughter, simply

because the mother is angry with you and wants to punish you or has a new man in her life?

In order to argue your point to the best of your ability in your statement, it will be necessary to think about how much time you used to spend with your child prior to the break-up.

If you were used to spending a lot of time together or played a 'hands-on' role with your child such as taking them to school or collecting them after school, or even if you just used to do activities with them that they liked and were used to, this is the type of important information that you should put in your statement.

You can state that you would like to continue playing the type of role you did with your child prior to the break-up. If this is no longer possible because you have moved away or are unable to make the same commitment as you did previously, you can make proposals that offer your child the same or similar time and opportunities to spend with you.

Mention how much your child enjoyed doing the activities or things they used to do with you. Explain that you are prepared to be flexible and recognise that your child will have certain routines that have been established for him or her. You intend not to disrupt them, but you want to balance their need for this routine with the importance of spending quality time with you—their father.

In the event that you were used to seeing your child daily, then it's entirely possible they are missing you tremendously. Again, it will be important to find out what your child wants, and then argue in accordance with their wishes, or if you think they do not really understand what is best for them, consider why it will be in their interest to see more of you than they currently do or say they want to.

The chances are good that if you have had a reasonably good relationship with your son or daughter, they will want to see more of you, having missed you greatly as a result of your separation.

You will need to talk with them gently about how they are feeling and whether they would like to see you more frequently. It is important to bear in mind that children are very receptive to your feelings and can be easily influenced by the way or manner in which you ask them about what they want.

Remember that you hold a very important position in your child's life and that for young children especially, they can look up to their parent as gods—in that they can see you as being incredibly powerful, as being all knowing, and as being able to do whatever you want.

Remember also that your child may be confused or unclear about what they want, and it may well be necessary to sensitively ask your child and talk to them frequently about their wishes and feelings, without making them feel pressured or that everything depends on what they say.

If you take the time to talk with them, watch their body language, be consistent and careful to let them know that you really want to know how they feel, you will gain within a short time a clearer sense of where they are at.

It will not be in your interests or your child's to force them to say something they don't want to because there is no guarantee that they will say what you want them to at the required time. More important in so doing, you will be harming them by imposing your wants on them.

Or, to put it another way, you will have crossed boundaries inappropriately, instead of allowing them to exercise their

views or free will, you will have instead imposed your views onto them.

Be conscious of the fact that young children may not have a sense of time, and if your child tells you that they would like to see you monthly or fortnightly when they clearly don't have a sense of time (and your ex-partner's proposal for your contact is similar or the same), then it is possible your child has been unfairly influenced.

Under such circumstances remain as calm as you can, set out your proposal or frequency of contact and explain as clearly as you are able to, that your child has no understanding of what a week, fortnight, or month is, so it would not be in their best interests to accept what they have stated without looking into the matter further.

Give or provide evidence which shows your child, given their age or level of understanding, does not know or understand what they are asking for.

If you have talked with your child about their feelings, they may well have said things to you which are inconsistent with seeing you fortnightly for example, and show that they are not clear about what they want.

As much as possible, find a measurement or common reference point that you and your child understand in terms of time. It may be that they go to Boy's Brigade or Girl Guide's, or do another activity, or even watch a programme they enjoy weekly or more frequently. Then you could, perhaps, find out whether they want to see you as often as they do this activity, or more or less often.

Once you have established this with your child, you are in a much better position to argue about what your child wants, and this can be more easily confirmed by the Family Court

Adviser if or when they speak to your child.

It is crucial not to come across as too dogmatic, but to show that you are both flexible and reasonable in your statement.

On a general point when writing your statement, where possible make it clear that you realise that your child has feelings, and that they are important to you, just as their safety and wellbeing are important. Mention also that you recognise that your child is not just yours and reflect this in the way you talk about him or her: Write for example that 'our' child is this or that.

It's a small thing but helps to place in the mind of the Family Court Adviser and the judge that you, at least, are thinking in this way. You can be quite sure that many of the parents seen in the family court do not do this and tend to communicate as though the child is theirs alone.

If you recognise your child has his or her own feelings and thoughts, which may be very different from those of yours or the other parent, and if you openly acknowledge that he or she is 'our' child, then you present yourself as someone who is more balanced and may be relied upon to act responsibly regarding their child.

As mentioned at the beginning of this chapter, it will be necessary to practice writing your statement and making your arguments many times to make sure that your statement is consistent with what your child needs most. If you are lacking in experience or confidence, why not enlist the help of others, who are not afraid of telling you how your statement reads or comes across.

You are not attempting to show perfect English, you simply need to be understood and to have argued any points from your child's point of view.

Along with the importance of being able to put across your views and arguments on paper, you also have to orally express your views and present yourself well at court.

CHAPTER SIX

VERBALLY REPRESENTING YOURSELF IN COURT

If you intend to verbally represent yourself during court hearings, there are a number of steps you need to take to prepare yourself to cope well with the matters that are likely to present themselves.

First and foremost, you need to have thoroughly thought out and talked through the circumstances relating to your dispute and your child's needs, ideally with someone neutral who has a clear understanding of what children need in order to achieve healthy development. (As many parents may not have access to or the support of someone who is skilled or knowledgeable in this area, a chapter of this book is devoted to offering you clear guidance regarding the type of care or parenting that children require, in order to develop towards healthy independence.)

I strongly advise you to take the time to read the chapter on 'Good Parenting' again and think about how the parenting you received, and that which you offer to your child, fits in or compares with some of the key indicators or skills described in that chapter.

I am suggesting that you think about the type of parenting you received from your parents. Unless you have gone out of your way to improve your parenting skills, you are highly likely to follow the same parenting style that your parents offered you.

In order to represent yourself as successfully as possible, you will have had to think about your child's wishes, feelings, and overall needs. You will literally have to learn to see things from the point of view of what's best for your child.

As one parent said to me the other day, this is far more challenging than it initially seems. Since all parents want to argue that they're doing what's best for their child, until they really look at what they are doing, they don't realise that it isn't always in their child's best interest.

Just as you need to practice writing a statement, you need to practice not only looking at what is in your child's best interest and being able to argue your case in line with your child's needs, you will also have to practice orally to communicate well in front of the judge or your ex-partner or anyone else in court.

To do this well requires a lot of practice, not least, because you do not get much time in court, and you will probably be heckled or interrupted by the other parent or whoever is representing them. For this reason, you have to be very familiar and confident about what you are saying, which really only comes about through continual practice.

It is also necessary for you to be aware that there is a code of conduct that you need to observe when in court.

Essentially, you should wait until the judge has asked you to speak before doing so. Be the calm and composed parent, and let the other side talk out of turn and become hot under the collar.

Your role is to comply with this code of conduct and marshal your emotions, so that you argue sensibly and present as favourably as possible.

The court room is not somewhere where everyone can speak at once, the judge has to maintain some order, so that he or she can hear the arguments and make sense of what's best for your child.

I know this is very difficult whilst you are under intense pressure at court. But this is precisely why I urge you to practice over and over again what you want to say, having regard for your child's wellbeing, such that you don't become flustered and lose the thread of your argument.

Let a friend play the part of your ex-partner or their legal representative and ask them to throw questions at you based on what you say is best for your child. Obviously, they will need to hear your arguments and proposal, and then play devil's advocate with you.

This is one of the best ways to prepare for your court case. Put yourself under the immense pressure you are highly likely to be under when you attempt to represent yourself at court. Do this over and over again whilst the other person tries to put you off by rubbishing what you are saying, by throwing questions at you, and generally by verbally making life difficult for you.

It would be a good idea to allow the person supporting you to have an idea of what your ex-partner is asking for, so that they can make it as real as possible for you.

Sometimes, depending on the court you come across, it could be the judge who is challenging what you have to say. If this is the case, it is all the more reason for you to prepare thoroughly, so that you can vigorously defend yourself verbally, by presenting your case in an expert manner.

The judge, your ex-partner, and their legal representative can all make you feel uncomfortable (although the judge would probably not wish to come across in this way), and this is another reason why you have to practice presenting your case.

It's a bit like an interview process, only what's at stake is far more important than an offer of work.

Let's look at a scenario in which Emma, the mother of Lucy, aged four, has recently separated from her partner, Steve.

Steve is the applicant and has applied for a Contact Order because he and Emma cannot agree on the level of contact Steve should have with Lucy. According to Steve, Emma had verbally agreed to him having fortnightly contact with Lucy for a few hours every other Saturday.

This worked reasonably well for a few months, but in recent months, contact has been sporadic because Emma claims Lucy has had a few children's parties that she has wanted to attend on Saturday and has had occasional illnesses.

However, Steve has realised that his difficulties regarding his contact with Lucy coincided with him introducing Lucy to his new partner.

In a scenario such as this, how can Steve best represent

himself at court to give himself the best chance of having regular contact with Lucy?

The first thing I would advise is that it was a mistake to introduce Steve's new partner to Lucy at this stage. This is a sensitive time when the break-up or separation is still quite new, and he is not sure how either Lucy or Emma feel about his involvement with someone new.

Even if it was Emma who severed the relationship with Steve, it's still a very vulnerable time, and he may not know Emma's views on him introducing Lucy to his new partner. As he sees far less of Lucy, he does not know how she will cope, or how she'll be affected by him doing so.

Let me be clear here: I am not saying Steve is wrong to have a new partner, since that is clearly Steve's right to do. But I would say that Steve needs to think about first putting Lucy's needs ahead of his own, and second, being cautious and strategic as regarding Emma and her feelings.

This second point about Emma is not about putting Emma's thoughts and feelings before your own, it is simply recognising the relatively powerful position Emma is in because Lucy lives with her.

Her position can allow her to make up all sorts of claims, which on the face of it could be true and focussed on Lucy's best interests, or alternatively, could be a pack of lies. The problem is it's not always simple to get to the truth of the matter, and Emma has much more opportunity to influence Lucy than Steve does.

I think Steve should acknowledge he's made a mistake and agree at this stage that he won't be asking his new partner to come into contact with Lucy until things are much clearer. When the new partner is an established part of his life, and

Lucy is far more settled and secure.

This may prompt Emma to allow him more frequent contact, but even if it doesn't, Steve can realistically argue that he is not asking for a lot of contact. Comparatively, this is a small level of contact weighed against the frequency with which he used to see Lucy.

Steve should argue in a manner totally consistent with whatever he wrote or documented in his statement. He should say she was used to seeing him more frequently than the fortnightly agreement he used to have with Emma. Then he can go on to say that he agreed to the fortnightly contact in order to show flexibility and not to cause further upset between him and Emma.

Steve could then explain that there were no real problems with that contact for a few months, until he made the mistake of bringing his new partner into the situation. He's now rectified this by agreeing not to bring her into contact for the foreseeable future with Lucy. He would now like a Contact Order to specify that he can have contact with Lucy for four hours every other Saturday, so as to ensure he sees Lucy without the problems of recent weeks.

In the event that Emma opposes the making of a contact order, saying she had concerns about Steve's punctuality as he kept her and Lucy waiting and that Lucy wanted to go to the parties in any case.

Steve could argue at the appropriate time, that is, when the judge gives him permission to speak, that there has never been any suggestion or indication that he has been late for contact, since if that was the case, it would have been stated before now. In addition, the fact that she has chosen to send Lucy to these alleged parties at a time when she was meant to be having contact with him, does rather suggest that

Lucy's contact with her father is not valued by Emma. Hence the need for a defined Contact Order.

I should point out at this point that Steve would appear to have a good chance of getting his Contact Order. But you need to bear in mind that the court has to consider the 'no order principle', which means that the court will not make an order unless it believes that making such an order would be better for Lucy than making no order at all.

One other thing I should add that will help you represent yourself in court is that together with how you conduct yourself in court, you should do your best to get there in good time and ensure that you are well dressed—treat going to court as if you are going to an interview. If you are a woman, wear conservative attire, a blouse and a skirt, or a dress; if you are a man, wear a dress shirt, tie, and suit, or at least a matching jacket and trousers.

It's all about making a good impression, and though it's not a massive point, you will present far better to the people that count if you do not arrive late, dressed in a pair of trainers and jeans, even if they are the latest fashion.

Dress formally and smartly in court and when you meet the Cafcass officer if you want to make the best impression, you can.

THE CAFCASS OFFICER'S ROLE

CAFCASS stands for the Child and Family Court Advisory and Support Service.

Almost inevitably when parents break-up and are unable to agree what is in the best interests of their child or children, they both hold the view that they know what is best for them.

As the court considers it crucial to obtain a clear, impartial, or independent view of what is in the child's best interests, they appoint a Cafcass officer or Family Court Adviser. Their role is to meet and interview the child and report their views to the court, so that the court is informed of the child's views, wishes, and feelings.

Most Family Court Advisers have a social work background and are considered to be skilled at working with all different types of children, who have a variety of complex needs. The Family Court Adviser or Cafcass officer is viewed as the expert in private law family proceedings, and, as a result, judges greatly value and listen to what Cafcass officers have to say or recommend.

Cafcass officers will often interview parents separately. They may ask a bit about the background from your point of view, and ask about how you and the other parent get along. They may enquire whether there has ever been any violence between you and your ex-partner, and whether there is any prospect of you both being able to work together to share your child's care.

They are likely to ask your views about what's best for your child, who played, if any, the major role in caring for your child when you lived together, and what you see as the best way forward.

You need to be keenly aware that whilst the Family Court Adviser is asking you these questions, that they are at the same time assessing your suitability and/or ability to care for your child.

The Family Court Adviser is extraordinarily busy, and it is unlikely they will spend much more than an hour with you.

After they submit their report to the court, you can request their attendance at court, in order to question them concerning their report.

The Cafcass reporter or officer is the person who will make recommendations about who your child should live with; who he or she should have contact with, and how often the contact should take place.

Prior to doing so, they will most likely complete a check with your local authority and the police to see if you are known to the authorities. They do this to make sure there are no safeguarding issues regarding you or the other parent's care.

Although the Cafcass officer is the court's expert, and they may have extensive experience working with a lot of children and families, it does not mean at all that they know what's best for your child.

I do not say this with any desire to stir up resentment within you towards whoever your Family Court Adviser is, since it is essential that you treat them courteously throughout.

My purpose in relaying this information to you is to help to 'put you in the picture' as much as possible.

Cafcass officers may not make recommendations which are in your child's true best interests, largely because they do not spend sufficient time looking at your child or the family's circumstances.

Your case is allocated only a certain amount of time and each Cafcass officer may have anywhere between 30 to 50 cases to manage at any one time. Given that this is the workload they carry, it is, perhaps, no surprise that they spend insufficient time on each case.

What this means in practice is that they will fail to pick up vital information, such as the child being manipulated by one of the parents to say something they don't really mean and is not in their best interests.

Or they will overlook the reality that for one of the parents the whole court case is not about the child at all, but instead merely a means to punish or abuse the other parent.

They may have missed or overlooked the most astounding pieces of information which would frankly concern people who were not even qualified social workers, and this has not happened because Cafcass officers are incredibly inept.

Instead, I would suggest this happens because Cafcass is financed by the government. Unfortunately, there are many more parents needing this service in comparison with the amount of resources available through Cafcass from the government. For families in conflict, the end result is that far too little time is spent working with the family, and hence some of the decisions made are ludicrous.

I know this will do little to fill you with confidence at a time when you are already fearful and stressed. But if you take the time to learn and practice some of the skills about children's needs, to think about your parenting, and how you will show you're placing your child's needs first on a consistent basis, you will have the best chance to get a favourable outcome. Practice and consider how you will present yourself to the Cafcass Officer and how you will present your arguments at court and give evidence. If you do so you will have a far better chance at obtaining your desired outcome (including whether you were represented by a solicitor or not).

PRESENTING YOURSELF TO THE CAFCASS OFFICER

If you are going to give yourself the best chance of obtaining a successful result at court, you need to recognise that the Cafcass officer is a highly influential figure in determining the outcome of your case and the circumstances relating to your child. You need to plan carefully the way you present yourself to him or her.

Apart from your child, the Cafcass officer is the most important person in deciding the result of your case. This is because the judge nearly always follows the recommendation by the Cafcass officer.

Whilst it is crucial to make a good impression on the Cafcass officer, your good impression may have been undermined by the way you have behaved at an earlier court hearing or by the way you have come across in your statement. Bear in mind also that a large proportion of your communication, like everyone else's is nonverbal and that much is picked up about who you are by your body language.

Children, for example, gather a lot of information about how you feel about someone, not so much by what you say about them or to them, but by the way you say it. Children notice matters such as your tone of voice, your facial expression, or whether you look at the other parent when the other parent is in your presence (and whether the other parent looks at you). It is information such as this that provides vital clues to your children about how you feel about the other parent.

But it does not just provide vital information for children about your real feelings, it also offers Cafcass officers crucial information about a range of matters, such as the type of parent you are, and what capacity you have to keep your child's thoughts and feelings, for instance, at the forefront of

your mind. Your capacity to work cooperatively with the other parent or present him or her in a reasonably positive light to your child and others can be decoded nonverbally.

Essentially, what I am attempting to impart to you is that your behaviour needs to be consistent throughout the proceedings from the beginning to the end. You need to be aware and think through, preferably with someone who is neutral (i.e., not on yours or the other parent's side) about the way you present, what you say about your ex-partner, and whether you perceive them as having any value to your child's life and future.

If you do not see the father or mother of your child as having any useful role in the life of your son or daughter, then this is very likely to affect the message you give your child about the other parent.

This type of information can be important for the Cafcass officer to gather, and it can have either a positive or negative impact on your chances of obtaining a successful outcome at court.

My advice to you is that you need to persistently be able to see things from your child's viewpoint, or be able to put yourself in your child's shoes.

Here the role of posing questions to yourself that you need to answer is key.

Ask yourself as many questions as possible:

- How would my child feel if they heard me saying negative things about their father?

- How would my child feel if they heard me calling their mother derogative or unpleasant names?

- What would be the impact on your child be if you become angry whenever you see them or hear the other parent's name mentioned?

- How would your child experience being dragged into arguments between you and the other parent?

- How might they feel if they were forced to take sides between the other parent and you?'

- What might be the impact on them of hearing continual arguments between you and the other parent?

- How might they feel if they were used as the main means of communication between you and the other parent?

The above are just a few of the questions that might prove very useful to begin to ask yourself to reflect on. They are designed to promote your thinking about your child's wishes, feelings, and needs.

However, many parents in the midst of parental conflict, emotional turbulence, and court proceedings are not able to answer these questions honestly or adequately. Also, they are often very likely to need the support of skilled neutral people to assist them in improving their understanding or insight into the needs and feelings of their children.

Sometimes, you can be helped to access the feelings your children may have by thinking about your own childhood experiences, and how you might have felt when your parents argued or said abusive things to one another.

I should state that being able to recognise your own memories about your childhood which were painful or harmful to you is likely to put you in a much better position to recognise the position your children sometimes feel placed in.

The problem is that it demands of you as a parent not only the ability to reflect insightfully about your childhood, but also to then empathise with your children accordingly to ensure they do not suffer the harm you may have suffered whilst dependent on your parents as a child.

The problem with some parents is that they do not recognise a difference between what they want, or what their needs are, and what their child's needs are.

It is vital that you as a parent realise the difference between your needs and those of your child's. They are not the same and as a good parent you will not only need to be aware of your child's needs, but you will have to be able to put their needs first and demonstrate your consistent ability to do so to the Cafcass officer.

The above information can really be summarised in four main points: (1) your capacity to reflect on how you come across, (2) your parenting and the parenting you offer your child, (3) your ability to empathise with your child's needs and prioritise them above your own, and (4) your capacity to consistently demonstrate your ability to do so throughout the proceedings.

In terms of your actual meeting or interview with the Cafcass officer, you need to see it as an interview or presentation, in that this is your chance to shine or present as the best parent possible without coming across as false or staged.

So, it is imperative that you plan and practice how you come across with someone who has an understanding of the types of questions that may be asked. Also, it is even more important that they can provide you with feedback over and over again about how you come across, until you can present yourself in a favourable way.

What's important is that, like verbally representing yourself at court, you get an opportunity to practice how you will speak to the Cafcass officer, how you will respond to their questioning of you, and how you show them that you are open to what they have to say, as opposed to coming across as closed. You need to think about how you will make them feel reasonably welcome in your home or comfortable in your presence if they interview you at their office.

It's perhaps a good idea to prepare some questions for the Cafcass officer, which not only highlights your concern or focus on your child's needs, but also gives the impression that you are ready and appreciative of advice they may offer you.

Although you are very likely to be extremely anxious about the meeting with the Cafcass officer, what you are unlikely to realise is that Cafcass officers are also frequently anxious about working with parents.

Cafcass officers have to cope with a considerable amount of stress and pressures. They are not just anxious because they are fearful about how you as a mother or father may respond to their questions and ultimately whatever recommendation they make. They are also highly pressurised by having to carry a very heavy workload, which places quite an intolerable burden on them as workers.

Now you should be aware of some of the pressures the Cafcass officer faces and their potential discomfort at interviewing you (even if they look confident to you). If you are wise, you will make their visit to you or your visit to their office as stress free as possible.

I do not mean to suggest that you go over the top and present a totally false impression of who you are, but it's

human nature to respond positively or favourably to people who have treated you pleasantly.

Do not underestimate the importance of being very polite, welcoming, and gracious to the Cafcass officer. For one thing, you can be certain that they are not always treated in this way, and frequently can't wait to get away from many of the parents they have to work with.

This is not because most parents are horribly aggressive by nature, but it's symptomatic of the stresses and fears most parents experience in relation to their children during the court process, which is emotionally draining on everyone.

If you want to give yourself the best chance of getting a favourable response from the Cafcass officer, spend almost as much time planning and practicing being pleasant to them as you spend thinking about your child's needs and how you will demonstrate this whilst being interviewed.

Most Cafcass officers are women, and so, if you are a father, you need to consider how you may come across to a female Cafcass officer.

The vast majority of Cafcass officers are social work trained or have a social work background, and being women, their generalised experiences or view of men may be that they have a tendency towards being violent, or, at the least, that men are less than sensitive to the needs of children.

Now, of course, they will know men who do not fit the stereotyped view mentioned above, but you need to bear in mind that women generally feel more threatened when working with men. This is to some extent because men may feel marginalised, and they can react in anger, which only tends to reinforce a negative view of men.

In a workforce which is predominantly made up of women and in a society where it is still presumed that women are best suited to caring for children, men are likely to have to work that much harder to receive the same or similar type of response as women.

This is probably not something the Cafcass officer is conscious of, but you as a father need to be very aware of it.

It would be nice to believe that discrimination or treating one group of people more favourably than another on the grounds of their gender no longer exists, but you would in my view be unwise to adopt this type of opinion.

What this means is that, as a generalisation, if you are a father, you are going to have to work much harder to convince the Cafcass officer that you are not in the least bit threatening, intimidating, or violent and are able to remain focussed on what is in your child's best interests.

I should add here, that if you have any history of abusing drugs or alcohol, or have any history of perpetrating violence, or abusive behaviour to women or children, then it is advisable to inform the Cafcass officer and demonstrate that you have taken steps to change this type of behaviour or lifestyle.

It may well be that the Cafcass officer already knows about your past because they are very likely to have completed a check on you with authorities, such as the police and social services at the outset of their involvement in the case.

That being the case, your chances of being successful, if you have such a history is much less likely, but it always looks better if you are able to acknowledge your past problems and are prepared to address them.

You really do not want to come across as being in denial about your past or as minimising the concerns identified, because then you will very probably be seen as posing a risk of harm to your child and that will not reflect positively on you.

You will have to develop the capacity to be really honest with yourself. You have to ask yourself if you were in the position of looking at two parents, with the focus of keeping the child's best interests at the forefront of your mind, and one parent had some history of abuse of drugs, or alcohol, or a history of violence to others, (that they have not received treatment or therapy for) whilst the other didn't, who would you feel more comfortable about as a parent?

So, in the interests of clarity, I would suggest to you, in the event that you have such a history, that you take steps to address any issues that could be viewed negatively by the Cafcass officer. In other words, if you have an anger management problem or an alcohol problem, make sure you enroll or attend a programme of treatment designed specifically to address the problem you face or have faced.

Do this as soon as possible, acknowledge past difficulties and problems, and, at all costs, be polite and as pleasant as possible to the Cafcass officer, whilst demonstrating your ability to remain focussed on the needs of your child throughout the interview and the proceedings.

Obviously, it would be unwise to get into an argument with the Cafcass officer, but if there is a matter you want to talk with them about, make sure you do so in an unthreatening manner.

Please bear in mind that depending on who you are, and who they are, although you may not perceive your actions to be in the least bit intimidating, this does not mean that your

actions and behaviour have been received in the way you have meant them to be.

This is another area in which you could benefit from the emotional and practical support of someone neutral, as opposed to someone who you perceive to be on your side. The problem here is that often it is precisely those people who have had a drug or anger management problem, for example, who do not recognise themselves as having a problem in that area of their life.

Yet, it is obvious to everyone else: the alcoholic who is adamant that he or she doesn't have an alcohol problem, the drug addict who claims not to be dependent on drugs, or the perpetrator of domestic violence who claims the violence is not his fault, and that the responsibility rests with the other partner or someone else other than them.

The bottom line is, if you really want to play an active and appropriate part in your child's life, you have to do your best to develop your insight, not only into your child's needs, but also your capacity to meet his or her needs. This means taking a long hard look at your actions and the role you have played in the past with your child.

It also means taking into consideration the role you have played with the other parent of your child. Whether you are a father or a mother, you cannot really claim to have done nothing to harm your child, or to have been the best parent possible if you have engaged in behaviour likely to harm the other parent.

Since the reality is that your child's wellbeing is linked very closely to the wellbeing of their parents. So, whether your child has observed your harmful actions or not, he or she will invariably be affected by them if their mother or father is harmed as a result.

I refer you to the earlier definition of harm, where it is acknowledged that children experience harm by seeing or hearing others being harmed or abused in some way.

It is important to state that many parents believe that their children have not witnessed or heard their arguments or conflicts when they actually have heard them. Even though the child may not have been in the same room at the time of the conflict, it does not mean that they have not heard it from another room, or have not picked up on the distress felt by one or both of their parents as a result of their quarrelsome relationship.

It pays to remember that children have been described as 'sponges' for a good reason. They are known to soak up everything they are exposed to, which includes toxic atmospheres.

If you are a black father, it may or may not come as a surprise to you to hear that some black men may be portrayed by the media as aggressive, violent, mad, or as a criminal for example.

Although some Cafcass officers may be very clued up and aware of the effect of factors such as racism on their individual practice, others may not be, and depending on where you live, the practices and level of awareness may differ widely.

In addition, it is perhaps worth remembering that when people are under stress as the Cafcass officer undoubtedly will be in 2013, that the conditions are ripe for unconscious behaviours to surface and decisions to be made from prejudices the Cafcass worker may not even be aware they are operating from.

Given that this may be the case, it is vital for black fathers

to do their best to positively challenge any of the negative stereotypes about black people and black males by remaining focussed on your child's needs and feelings and being as affable and courteous as possible.

If you have an issue or matter you feel the need to discuss with the Cafcass officer, choose carefully how you bring up the matter and ensure that it demonstrates your ability to think unselfishly about your child's welfare or best interests.

The problem that some parents show to their detriment is their anger and inability to focus on matters other than their frustration with the other parent or with issues that solely concern them and have little if anything to do with the welfare of their child.

On a final note, where possible, practice talking about the other parent in a reasonably positive way. Remember you may hate their guts currently, but they are the mother or father of your child and as such are a very important person in your child's life.

Remember also that you are just one of many cases that the Cafcass officer holds at the same time. It can be very comforting for the officer to hear at least one out of numerous parents talking about the other parent with some kind of respect and a recognition that, despite your differences, you realise that the other parent is important in your child's world—just as you are.

In the event that you do not agree with the recommendations made by the Cafcass officer, you are within your right to request that they attend court, so that you can question them whilst they are in the witness box.

This brings us to the subject of giving evidence at court.

Many parents do not have to do so because their court case ends prior to this becoming necessary, but should you ever need to give evidence in court, then you will need to prepare thoroughly and practice repetitively the vital skills mentioned in the next chapter.

CHAPTER SEVEN

GIVING EVIDENCE AT COURT

Giving evidence in court means that you will be asked to be seated in the witness box and be sworn in. Depending on whether you have a religious faith or not, you will either be asked to swear on the bible or affirm.

If giving evidence in court concerning your family court case, it is advisable for you to prepare thoroughly.

Beforehand, you will need to read the other parent's statement and your own, as well as the Cafcass officer's report at least once, but if needs be more than once, making notes to aid your memory as you do so.

Depending on the way you learn best, it might be a good idea to write down the various points you want or need to make and commit them to memory, so that when you are asked certain questions, your mind does not go completely blank as it can do whilst under pressure in the witness box.

 how2become

You need to see giving evidence at court as your chance to present the evidence or information you want to give, and it's your opportunity for the court to see what type of person you are.

 Although it might feel like you are in the witness box for a long time, it's unlikely to be for much longer than half an hour, unless there's an awful lot of evidence to go through. However, within that time, you need to present yourself as a credible witness.

What this means is that you need to be believable. Even if you are not able to answer all the questions that are fired at you by your ex-partner's solicitor or barrister to your satisfaction, the absolute worst thing to do is to lie or make false allegations.

You need as much as possible to be yourself and to behave as naturally as possible, provided that you are not someone prone to making wild allegations about the other parent or others.

Immediately prior to giving evidence, it's vital to your performance that you make yourself as calm and relaxed as possible.

Following being sworn in, you'll be asked to sit down.

Take some deep breaths and position yourself in the seat as comfortably as possible.

When answering questions, although you will be asked questions by the other parent's barrister or legal representative (unless like you—your ex-partner is representing themselves), you should address your answers or responses to the judge, as it is he or she who needs to hear your answers first and foremost.

Be mindful of the way solicitors or barristers will ask their questions. Sometimes they will begin by asking harmless questions. Do not be afraid to answer these questions as appropriate. If asked a simple question and the obvious answer is for example, yes. Then say 'yes' as there is no harm or prejudice to you in saying so. On the contrary, if you appear to dither, you will appear less credible in the judge's eyes.

A tactic that some legal representatives use is to lull you into a false sense of security by asking you simple questions that you can't help but agree with. They may ask you four or five simple questions all of which you will have to say yes to, and then, without warning, they may sneak in a question you will be forced to think about or that you don't agree with.

If they do this, take some seconds to think about the answer that you want to give. Do not feel overly pressured because you have not been able to answer immediately. You do not score points by rattling off answers swiftly as though you were in a race. The object for you is to come across as believable, and to do so at times, it is necessary to think deeply about the answer you give.

It is much better to take your time and answer the questions honestly and sensibly, than to rush through and say something you will later regret or which makes you appear less credible.

Also at times, the other parent's solicitor or barrister will ask you a question which appears to you to strengthen their case but is nevertheless true or for the most part true.

If you answer these questions truthfully, even though they seem to cast a dark shadow on your case, the judge will at least see you as honest, which will favourably reflect on your character with him or her.

If they are partly true questions, explain that this is the case. Say, for example, 'I agree that this, that, and the other thing are true. However, in my opinion, this is not always the case because ...' And then go on to argue why this is not completely true.

Notice that I have used the words 'in my opinion'. You could equally use the words 'in my experience'.

Often legal representatives will present a small part of the overall picture of what's been going on as though it were the whole truth, and it will be down to you to present or explain the overall situation.

For instance, they may say that Mr Brown—the father— has contacted you on numerous occasions in an effort to come to an agreement about reasonable contact with his daughter. 'Isn't that true?'

Your response may then need to be something like this: 'It's true that Mr. Brown has contacted me on many occasions, and he always says his reason for making contact has to do with our daughter. However, first, I have never stopped him from having contact with our daughter'.

'Second, the frequency with which he makes contact seems to me to be obsessive, since I have over seventy text messages within the last couple of months'.

Mr Brown's legal representative may then counter that he's felt forced to contact you so frequently because you refuse to communicate with him and come to an agreement about contact.

At which point, you might say something to this effect: 'I will repeat that I have never stopped him from having contact, nor have I attempted to regulate its frequency. I have, however,

refused to answer his obsessive text messages, because he bombards me with them. They are harassing and abusive in nature, and the content of them has nothing to do with his contact with our daughter'.

At which point, you may wish to back up your statement with producing a transcript of a selection of Mr Brown's many abusive texts to you.

So whilst his solicitor has attempted to portray you as being obstructive to his contact, you have defended yourself by explaining the wider picture, taking into account the context of his abusive texts as the reason for your refusal to communicate with him. You have also backed up your claim with documented proof of his abusive texts and provided information which pours considerable doubt on his claim that he wants to come to an agreement regarding contact with his daughter.

Giving evidence at court under oath is extremely stressful for the vast majority of people who are asked to do so. And just like writing your statement and verbally representing yourself at court, you will need to rehearse and practice these skills over and over again, until you are comfortable or feel more prepared to give evidence.

You have to realise that giving evidence is very much a mental and emotional battle of which you have to remain in control.

Solicitors or barristers cross-examining you will try to rattle you, sometimes by speaking to you in unpleasant and accusatory tones. Do not let this upset or distract you, expect it.

Your task is to remain calm and focussed at all times on your child. When you are asked questions, you must always keep your child at the forefront of your mind.

Do not under any circumstances allow yourself to be drawn into an argument with your opponent's solicitor or barrister, as this will jeopardise your ability to respond sensibly and as practiced, and impact potentially negatively on your presentation.

You may be asked questions such as 'It would be true to say that you really don't like the mother very much, do you?'

Now whilst this may very be true, it would be unwise to just agree with what you are being asked. Instead of just saying, 'Yes, I really don't like her', it would be far wiser to say something similar to this: 'It would be true to say that we have had some serious differences, which have been upsetting to both of us and our child. But she is the mother of our child, and I'd prefer it if we could get along for our child's sake'.

What this does is present you as both reasonable, conciliatory, and most important, focussed on your child's wellbeing, since too many parents in those circumstances fail to recognise the disastrous impact on their child. It also suggests you have the ability to recognise that she has also been hurt by whatever has gone on between both of you.

In other words, it demonstrates that you have the capacity to think about others and not just yourself.

Many parents are not only unable to see things from their child's point of view, they are also unable to accept that they are not the only people who have been hurt.

If you had simply agreed with what you were asked, although you were being truthful, you would not have presented as someone who was able to keep their child uppermost in their thoughts.

Sometimes barristers may ask you two questions at once.

My advice to you is to take your time and answer them one at a time, taking time to think about your answer, and that your answers don't contradict each other.

You have to think carefully about what you either say in evidence or have stated in your statement, and your arguments need to be consistent.

If, for example, you have claimed in your statement or during giving evidence that you are worried, given his obsessive behaviour, that he may be mentally unwell, then you should be prepared for a question like: 'Well, if you think Mr. Brown is mentally unwell, why on earth would you allow him to see your daughter whenever he likes? Isn't the truth of the matter that you know he's a devoted father?'

Your reply might then be: 'In the past, he was not a bad father, but in recent months, I have grown concerned about his state of mind. The reason I have not sought to curtail his contact with our daughter is because I fear his behaviour would become worse, and our daughter does look forward to seeing him'.

Your response explains to the court your dilemma in managing this situation and demonstrates your ability to consider your child's needs in the midst of the concerning behaviour from the other parent.

When preparing for giving evidence, it's really essential that you know your own statement, the other parent's, and the Cafcass officer's report very well.

It often helps to jot down the important or salient points you wish to make, which back up or support the proposals you are recommending. You do not have to write your

points down in note form if you are more comfortable with presenting your arguments diagrammatically or in any other way. What is important is that when it comes to you giving your evidence, you are comfortable and confident about what you are saying.

As mentioned under the chapter 'Verbally Representing Yourself At Court', it will help you tremendously if you have someone who can throw questions at you that you have to answer and who can give you feedback on your responses. You cannot overestimate the importance of constant practice and preparation.

The question that you have to keep asking yourself and answering is — 'How is what I'm saying or proposing in my child's best interests overall?'

If you really can't answer that question satisfactorily, you'd better start over again.

You should go over your statement very carefully, as if you were working for the other parent. The purpose of doing so is to spot any inconsistency or areas that have not been properly thought through, which can be exploited by your opponent or expose you to criticism.

Be aware of the strengths as well as the weaknesses of your arguments. If you do this properly, you will know where your argument is most vulnerable and likely to come under attack. You will also know where the strengths of your argument lie and the resulting benefits to your child.

As well as giving evidence, you may want to question both the other parent and the Cafcass officer in the event that you or the other parent are unhappy about her report and/or her recommendations.

Having a list of pre-prepared questions to ask the Cafcass officer and the other parent will be highly advantageous to you, particularly since you will be very unused to this role and will need to be as organised as possible.

It will be a good idea to come to court with a pen and note pad, so that you can make a note of their responses, rather than leaving it all to your memory. It will be necessary for you to do a certain amount of thinking on your feet when questioning the Cafcass officer and the other parent. This is one of the reasons it will be imperative that you know extremely well what they have written in their reports and statements.

Whilst representing yourself at court or giving evidence, you should observe the code of conduct mentioned and follow the judge's directions.

Once the Cafcass officer, you, and the other parent have given your evidence and have been cross-examined, the judge will let you know the outcome of the case and any orders he intends to make.

CONCLUSION

The court system as regards private family law in this country is frankly, in my view, extremely poor. The service offered to children and parents at a very critical period in their lives is astonishingly inadequate, and this is not, in my opinion, because the people involved in providing the service are uncaring.

It is simply that the service is insufficiently resourced. Even with the best will in the world given the sheer number of competing problems and political agendas, it seems unlikely that in the near future, this issue will be prioritised by the government.

As a consequence, the courts' and the Cafcass officers' time is spread too thinly over the cases that present themselves at court, with the result that many children are not offered anything like a quality service. This situation has left many parents traumatised and bitter, and, in the end, damaged by the service.

The knock on effect or repercussions are quite obvious, if parents are harmed by the process, inevitably children are harmed as a result. I am not aware of any relevant research undertaken in this area, but suspect that the impact on society is far larger than immediately realised.

What you also need to realise is that, at the end of the case, if you have been granted the order you wanted, this, by no means, indicates that any problems you were facing with your ex-partner are over, because the other parent may decide not to abide by the order.

If your ex-partner ignores the order, the only choices you have are to put up with things, try to negotiate with them, or bring the matter back to court and go through the whole

process again. You can consider calling the police to enforce the order, but in my experience, this is not fruitful, and as a result, you can see why some parents feel they have no choice but to return to court.

The court system rarely if ever solves your family problems, but if you have to go to court, the better prepared and equipped you are to manage the situation adequately, the better for you and your child. Particularly, if you have to go to court on successive occasions.

After your family court case has at last come to an end, whether you feel the outcome was unsuccessful or successful, no matter how you feel about the other parent and what the Cafcass officer or the court did or did not do, you have to get on with your life and make your life and your child's as happy a life as you can make it.

Whilst the court process is however ongoing, this is your opportunity to put your time to the best use and **PRACTICE, PRACTICE, PRACTICE**.

I cannot overstate how vital it is for you to prepare thoroughly for everything you do, from learning about what good parenting entails to writing your statement to meeting the Cafcass officer to representing yourself in court and giving evidence.

As the concerned parent of your child, you know better than anyone else exactly what is at stake when you go to court.

Given the gravity of the situation, many parents seek certainty or as much certainty as possible in a world where little if anything is certain.

The best assurance I can offer you is the assurance gained from knowing that you have prepared diligently for your court case.

There is an awful lot of work involved, and I have done my best to highlight the knowledge and skills you need to develop and practice repeatedly to give yourself the best chance of achieving the outcome you want at court.

However, it is far beyond the scope of this book or any other to deal with every possible scenario your family court case may involve.

In the light of this, should you need further support, you can email me at familycourtcoaching@hotmail.co.uk.

Michael D. Watson
Family Court Coach

how2become

Visit www.how2become.com for more business titles and career guides.

www.how2become.com